CONFESSIONS *of a*
MILLIONAIRE'S
MISTRESS

CONFESSIONS *of a*
MILLIONAIRE'S MISTRESS

AVA REILLY

ALLEN&UNWIN

SYDNEY • MELBOURNE • AUCKLAND • LONDON

Author's note: Some names and identifying details in this book have been changed to protect the anonymity of the persons involved.

First published in 2015

Allen & Unwin
83 Alexander Street
Crows Nest NSW 2065
Australia
Phone: (61 2) 8425 0100
Email: info@allenandunwin.com
Web: www.allenandunwin.com

Cataloguing-in-Publication details are available
from the National Library of Australia
www.trove.nla.gov.au

ISBN 978 1 76011 203 5

Set in 14/19.5 pt Granjon LT Std by Bookhouse, Sydney
Printed and bound in Australia by Griffin Press

10 9 8 7 6 5 4 3 2 1

To all the broken souls who never learnt to recover their stolen innocence; to anyone who ever dared to be different; and to anyone who followed their heart no matter how much it hurt.

Contents

#BeforeHugh

My first confession was posted online in November 2013. I'll never forget the feeling I had when I finally clicked 'post' on my Facebook page. A thousand people from all over the world and all walks of life had 'liked' my page and were excited to read my first confession. I'm not sure what their expectations were, nor perhaps what mine were, in terms of what I would reveal, and one of my biggest fears was that I would slip up somewhere and forget to change the names of the people I was writing about. This would be a disaster; I really don't want anyone to get hurt. I'm doing this for me. I needed to get a lot of things off my chest and desperately needed a release from the pain that had consumed my soul. The response from my first confession was overwhelming, and to this day I still cannot believe that the demand for more has been so high—so much so that I'm now sitting here writing this book! I've always wanted to write a book, but every time I started I found myself deleting each paragraph, unsatisfied with my efforts. I contacted a friend of mine who is deservedly an award-winning author and asked her to write my book for me, but the more I wrote the more I realised that the passion I couldn't quite find for writing had been missing because I hadn't been writing from the heart. After an earth-shattering betrayal, as I tried to gather the pieces of my broken heart, I decided it was time to write . . . my confessions.

I'm alone in my apartment, sitting in my bedroom with a glass of white wine, at the desk that my late grandfather built for me. In all the years since he passed I have cherished it more than anything else. It was the last gift I received from him. I'm surrounded by memories . . . but only the good ones. It has taken me many years to be able to break away from all negativity in my life and learn to breathe easily, and writing this book has been part of the process.

I am now in my early twenties and, although I still have many demons to fight, I feel I have become successful in my own right. I work with a roster of internationally renowned celebrity clients, and the insecurities I felt about this industry and the people in it have almost all but disappeared. It has taken time and a lot of soul-searching for me to realise that this is the path that I was destined to travel. I have no regrets in life, and I never like to fall asleep at night wondering 'What if'. I think I am quite a strong person and although my personal life hasn't always turned out the way that I wanted it to, I stick by the decisions I have made to this day.

It took me a little while to realise that the key to my happiness is to own my mistakes and turn them into life lessons, but luckily I believe that it is never too late to learn.

To paint a picture of how I feel right now, I want you to listen to a song called 'These Days' by Powderfinger—the lyrics explain why the journey I embarked on was something that I never expected; with every twist and turn I found myself learning that you should never judge a book by its cover.

•

There is one story in particular from my life before Hugh that I know I need to share to give you an understanding of why I made some of the decisions I did about our relationship. I will never use them as an excuse; however, I think it will allow you to have a clear idea of why the path I travelled down was one I felt was the only choice I had left.

I had a series of not-so-nice men in my life within a short period of time but one man stands out as the one who left me the most vulnerable.

I met Richard just after I began working for my current employer. He was a potential business contact with whom I had arranged a meeting. The first time I spoke to him over the phone I thought his voice sounded quite attractive. I was intrigued to find out what he looked like.

When he arrived for our afternoon meeting I was alone in the office. The moment I laid eyes on him, I realised that the voice on the phone didn't match the person standing in front of me. This man was tall, dark, skinny and anything but handsome. It wasn't necessarily his physical appearance that turned me off so much as a look in his eyes that set me on edge. He was lovely and polite, and our meeting went well, but I couldn't shake that initial feeling that something felt off about him.

I sent a bit of work his way over the following weeks and months and we built a good relationship. Eventually we became quite good friends, but nothing more than that.

Meanwhile, my boss had noticed that Richard and I were getting along quite well and tried to encourage me to go out to dinner with him. I couldn't explain to her that I didn't feel comfortable being alone with him when I didn't have much reason to feel that way other than my gut instinct.

Richard kept asking me out to dinner over the course of nine months but I kept making up excuses as to why I couldn't go. Sometimes I tried to convince myself that my first impression must have been wrong; he was always so lovely to me and treated me very well, so I tried to force myself to like him the way he liked me, but it never worked.

Then one night Richard happened to call me when I was extremely upset, and he asked me what was wrong.

I was so vulnerable and really needed to talk to someone about what I was feeling. I spent so much time hiding my emotions from other people, but now it was impossible to keep it in. I told him that I had been abused when I was younger and that I had just come into direct contact with the man who had abused me. I didn't go into detail, but I told him just enough for him to understand why I was so upset. I explained that I wanted to join the police force and specialise in the field of child protection. At this stage in my life I felt that it was my calling because of the abuse I had suffered, but I wasn't entirely sure I would be able to handle the stresses of the job day in, day out.

While Richard was initially quiet, it wasn't long until he began asking me unexpected questions: about what my emotions had been like at the time of my abuse, how much damage it had done and how I felt about the situation now. I was distraught and initially felt that there was no way I could continue the conversation, but on the other hand no one had ever asked me that before and I saw an opportunity to get a lot off my chest. By the end of our call I was exhausted, and couldn't wait to go to sleep and forget about the horrible day I had endured.

Richard began calling me more often and asking me out, which I found odd but my colleagues and boss found quite amusing. They couldn't understand why I didn't want to go out with him. One afternoon he even called my boss and asked her to convince me to go out with him. She knew that I trusted her opinion and tried to put in a good word for him, but at this point I knew it was never going to happen.

A few weeks later we were putting together a big event that Richard offered to help out with. As much as I didn't want this to happen, we needed the help, and my boss thought he would do a great job.

Richard had sensed that something was off with me early in the day, and when we were finally alone together he asked me what was wrong. I didn't feel like I could tell him that he creeped me out, as he had begun telling me how much he loved me, so I tried to avoid his questions.

As I turned to pass him he grabbed my wrist with such force that I winced from the pain.

'*Never* touch me again,' I snapped, before ripping my arm from his grip and walking around him to exit the room.

That was the last straw for me. Richard continued to chase me, no matter what I did, but I was well and truly put off by his behaviour. I saw no reason to be civil with him any longer. As it turned out, he soon revealed his true colours to other people as well.

One afternoon when I had a day off my boss unexpectedly showed up at my front door. She told me that she had seen Richard in the office that morning, and they were in the middle of a friendly conversation when he revealed that he had been to prison. He hadn't gone into any detail about why, but she told me she knew it wasn't good. She felt terrible about having tried to convince me to go out with him.

My stomach was in knots. I had no idea how I was going to get away from him. Now I feared that upsetting him might make him angry, and I didn't know what that would trigger.

I knew I had to solve this once and for all. After my boss left I texted Richard to confront him about what he had told her, and to tell him that I didn't want to continue our personal relationship. After hundreds of messages back and forth I finally received the response that would shatter my world.

'Don't judge me until you know all of the story. You're right Ava, I went to jail for underage sex offences against my daughter. This kills me to have to say this again, not only to myself but to you, too. There were many factors that led me to this happening and until recently I didn't understand what they were. I've done programs in gaol and another out of gaol, I've been to counselling since I was released and have tried to fit back in to society as best as possible. People like you and your family make that possible for me. As a young boy from the age of 6 I was abused by a girl down the road, when I was 12 I was interfered with by a teacher and then raped by a teacher when I was 14. Later that year I was raped by my mate's mother then father, and then by him. None of this was ever reported and you are the first person I have told outside of my programs. I am not making excuses for myself,

I am merely stating fact. I put my hand up and pleaded guilty because it was the only thing I could do that would make things seem remotely right. I am terribly ashamed of what I had done and went to gaol without complaint. I disgraced myself and my family. This will not happen in my life again: that is a promise I can make you!

'This is the main reason why I stopped asking you out. You could not be seen in an intimate relationship with a person who was convicted of the very offence that you want to work to prevent. Above all, I want you to know that at that point in time my concerns were for you and your career in the police force. When you told me what happened to you my heart stopped and I wasn't sure what I could say to you, so I called on what I learned about myself and told you that it was not your fault. And it is true, darling, it's not your fault. Even though I've done this I despise the crime. I would only be too willing to help you further, but that is of course your choice. There is so much more to talk about but this can't be done by text in this manner. Ring me when u are ready—but I would rather see you to explain.'

I instantly felt violated—just holding my phone with those words on the screen made me feel ill. He knew everything I had been through, and I felt as though he had used my pain as his sick way of trying to find out how his daughter felt after what he had done to her.

It was in the aftermath of this text message that I decided to swear off men forever. How could I ever believe that any man was going to be honest with me, and be worthy of my trust? I felt that if I let anyone in I would end up betrayed and broken again. I only ever saw Richard once after that but I refused to even acknowledge him.

So many men in my life had left me scarred beyond repair, and because of them I knew the next man who came into my life would have to be someone pretty special to be able to scale the walls that I had built up to protect myself. They had to be able to prove themselves, because I wasn't sure I could survive another heartbreak.

#FirstConfession

#COAMMPlaylist:

'Infatuation'

Christina Aguilera

The morning after I met Hugh, I woke up thinking I must have imagined what had happened; it couldn't possibly have been true. I managed to convince myself that what I had felt around him had to be some form of crazy emotional surge, that my imagination was playing tricks on me. There was no way a man so powerful, well respected and well known would have even the slightest interest in a nobody like me. Even if what I had felt *was* real, it would certainly have been unrequited. As I lay in bed questioning my sanity, I felt the familiar butterflies in my stomach that had been set loose hours earlier as he and I had texted late into the night. Before I had fallen asleep I replayed everything in mind, as if I was watching a movie. Surely I misread the signs? As much as I tried to convince myself, I knew deep down that something *had* happened.

•

It was the biggest professional opportunity of my career. I was just starting to reach my stride in my role as a public relations manager for worldwide celebrities and brands when a contact—let's call him Dario—gave me my first lead; I couldn't pass it up. Dario had arranged a table at an inaugural event held in one of the biggest venues in Australia, and he asked if I would like two seats—it would, he said, be a fantastic opportunity to get a taste of what was to come if I truly wanted to go down this PR path. I was over the moon, and I jumped at the chance.

When I first entered this industry I was very naive but I knew two things: I had to keep my wits about me, and the right first impression could really give me the foot in the door that would otherwise take years to achieve. I have always been the type of person to go after the things I want, and I wanted this career. I am not conventional by any stretch of the imagination, and I have always liked to be different, and I knew that this career would suit me perfectly. Little did I realise where it would lead me, and to this day I have never regretted my decision. Looking back, I may be more mature and have seen things that have made me wiser, but I still believe that there is no better career than the media and entertainment industry . . . but it is not for the faint-hearted.

It wasn't until after I arrived at the lunch event that I realised just how important it was, and how influential the guests were. The patrons were a healthy mix of celebrities, media, agents, publicists and the who's who of the entertainment industry. I instantly felt self-conscious and out of place—I was, after all, only eighteen—but I took solace in the fact that one of my bosses had accompanied me. We sat at our table surrounded by people we barely knew but who immediately welcomed us to their group. They knew Dario, and because we were his guests they were nothing short of polite. We each had a celebrity at our table and this made me feel a little more unnerved because I had no idea if we were supposed to interact with them or if we should leave them alone. Some of them looked like they would rather be anywhere else—I even caught one of them playing Doodle Jump on his iPhone—but the man seated next to me at our table was charming and kind.

After the initial speeches, three-course lunch and charity auction I finally began to relax and feel that I was there for the right reasons. Once the official parts of the luncheon were complete we were all free to mingle, and I knew I had to make the most of my opportunity; I had once been told to 'fake it till you make it' and I planned to do just that. I made a beeline for the head honchos in the media and a few key celebrities. I planned my moves, ensuring I entered conversations with the right celebrities and then exited at just the right time, always leaving a memorable impression on those I knew could help my career progression. What I couldn't realise at the time was that my efforts had exactly the effect I desired, and that soon the people in that room would come to see me as part of the inner circle—at the say-so of a man I didn't even know existed . . . yet.

A week after the event Dario called me. It wasn't strange for him to call me, but this time was different. He was in a hurry and dispensed with the usual pleasantries and got straight to business: a heads-up on something big coming up. He told me I needed to call a man by the name of Hugh Montgomery, a businessman who had a number of high-profile clients both in Australia and overseas who would need PR assistance on an upcoming project.

'Get on to it, Ava,' Dario told me. 'You have what it takes, and you have the element of surprise on your side. It hasn't hit the media yet; he'll sit up and pay attention because you know something that isn't a matter of public knowledge.'

I didn't realise the extent of this man's pull or even who he was but Dario explained briefly that he was well known within the entertainment industry: possibly the most prominent in the field. Deciding not to let the opportunity go to waste, I called his mobile and, with sweaty palms and a nervous shake in my voice, I left a message asking him to call me. I didn't expect to hear back from him, so I went on with my day as usual, not thinking anything more about Hugh Montgomery.

That night at seven o'clock he called me back, cool, calm and collected with a velvety smooth voice that instantly made me melt. When he introduced himself I froze, wondering what the hell I was supposed to say. Dario had not prepared me for the fact that he sounded like a god! I attempted to maintain some level of decorum despite my nerves, determined not to blow my opportunity. I decided it was time to fake it till I made it, leading him to believe I knew more about what was going on than I really did, and in turn without even realising it he gave me all the information I needed. I really wanted this account, and I knew that I would be able to back up my promises. I was determined to prove myself, and I didn't even realise that I had shifted into autopilot work mode and blocked everything else out. He told me he was flying into town the next day, and he asked to meet with me to discuss possible opportunities.

We arranged to meet the next night for dinner at his hotel. I was nervous, but more importantly I was excited. I was eighteen years old and about to meet with one of the most influential people in the country. Hugh had given me the time of day and I felt on top of the world. I knew I was on to something huge—I could feel it in the depths of my soul—but little did I know how significant this was going to become both professionally and personally. My life was about to turn upside down and there was nothing I could do to stop it.

•

The next day I was set to meet Hugh. Something in the morning air had me a little off balance, but I kept repeating my new mantra: *fake it till you make it*. Something deep down inside told me that I didn't need to be worried, but I didn't trust my instinct, so I invited my boss and her husband to attend.

When we arrived at the hotel to meet Hugh for dinner, the concierge told us the hotel did not have a guest under that name. Suddenly I was worried. I had received a phone call from this man and yet I hadn't even googled him until ten minutes before I got out of the car at the hotel. His name is so well known across the industry that a Google search brings up well over a million results; he is the biggest powerbroker in the industry and yet he was meeting *me*. I was still in shock but I knew I had to be the consummate professional to get him to take me seriously—and here I was, suddenly panicking and thinking that I had made a huge mistake.

My boss and her husband excused themselves to use the bathrooms and as I stood in the lobby of one of the grandest hotels I had ever seen, I felt a shiver run down my spine and an electric pull forced me to look to my left: the glass doors had opened and I watched in awe as a middle-aged, broad-shouldered, tanned man dressed in Armani with a

16

supreme air of confidence walked in, talking heatedly on his phone before ending the call abruptly. As I tried not to stare, he began to walk towards me. Something about the way he walked, talked and held himself drew me in. I can't say it was necessarily his looks that attracted me, but there was an air of mystery about him, something that told me he was a lethal cocktail of danger and restraint that would be difficult for any woman to ignore. Clearly he was a lady's man, his charisma oozing out across the room and hitting me at full force. It seemed that at any moment my jelly legs would give way and I would pass out, but I forced myself to focus. This man screamed class and everything else I felt I lacked in that moment. In an instant I knew it was him, even though I had never laid eyes on him before.

He walked straight over to me and as he held out his hand I saw a warm and genuine smile spread across his face and touch his eyes. There was something in his eyes that told me there was more to him than his name and reputation. I was intrigued, I was nervous, but predominately I was left breathless; his gaze penetrated the walls I had developed to protect myself over the years. He made me feel vulnerable. It was as if, at our first meeting, we recognised each other—and it scared the hell out of me. I had to look away. He breathed, 'Good evening, Ava' and at the exact time I said, 'Hello, Hugh.' For the first time I could remember, I found myself lost for words.

Suddenly my mind went blank; I didn't even realise that I was shaking his hand, his firm grip holding my own. I couldn't look away from his eyes, and the smile on his face disappeared as his head tilted to the side and he started to say, 'I think I've met you—' at the very moment my boss and her husband emerged and joined us. The static that shot up my arm as the touch of his hand left mine jolted me back to reality, and I finally found my voice to make introductions.

He asked us to wait for him in the bar while he checked in to the hotel, and as I turned away my mind was in a complete haze. Before I knew what was happening, my heart sped up as he grabbed my elbow and spun me around to look straight into my eyes. In a split second he stopped himself from whatever it was that he was going to do and walked away, leaving me standing there utterly confused. What the hell was going on? Why did I feel like I had seen him before? Like I knew him? It was the strangest feeling, like an electric shock had vibrated through me each time he touched me.

Twenty minutes later he joined us at a secluded table at the back of the hotel restaurant. He was refreshed, changed, and as he passed me a deliciously clean, sophisticated scent penetrated my nostrils. Behind Hugh was a mirror, and in its reflection I could see I was flushed—but I couldn't explain why. I felt fine, just a little confused. I kept quiet during the meal while business was discussed, which is quite unlike me, but I felt like my brain had been fried. He was sitting opposite me and I tried my hardest not to look him in the eye because I have been told that my eyes always give me away, and I was afraid of what they would reveal—I couldn't even figure out what was going on inside my head. The more I saw of him throughout the night the more I knew that he was trouble, and the only thing I could think was *Where is the closest exit?* He had serious charisma and I found it unbelievably alluring; there was just something that forced me to keep sneaking glances in his direction. Every time I looked at him I caught him watching me.

When I look back, I think that there were so many warning signs about what was surely to happen between Hugh and me. At that first dinner I was mesmerised but I also found myself despising him, and I don't even know why. Perhaps my insecurity and nerves were winning out. I knew that there was no way he would be interested in me—I could only imagine the types of women who entertained him and I certainly didn't think I fitted the bill—but I couldn't deny the energy that flowed between us. My palms were sweaty as I sat there trying my hardest not to look at him, staying uncharacteristically quiet, afraid of sounding like a fool.

About an hour into the meeting I felt his foot touch mine. I was so on edge that any connection with him felt like lightning striking me. I pulled my foot away as another shot of electricity ran through my body; I couldn't look at him and I found myself holding my breath. Moments later he apologised and asked whose foot he had kicked; I said it was fine and moments later found his foot began to tap mine. With each tap I felt like I was being tasered: mildly painful and yet I didn't want him to stop. I snuck a glance in his direction just once, to try to understand what he was trying to achieve, but he wasn't giving anything away.

At one point the conversation turned to music and he asked me who my favourite band was. I was able to mutter, 'Matchbox Twenty', to which my boss's husband said, 'Oh, who cares about them?' with a laugh. Hugh immediately piped up, saying, 'Well, obviously *she* does,' in an oddly protective tone. The table fell silent. I had never had someone stick up for me like that, especially not a stranger. It intrigued me that this man was sitting here defending me over something that seemed so insignificant but actually meant so much to me.

A little later Hugh asked where the bathrooms were and I offered to show him. We walked together in silence, and as we rounded the corner I almost jumped as his hand rested on the small of my back. When we reached the bathrooms Hugh asked if I wanted to join him. He stood looking at me, deadly serious, while my brain struggled to catch on that he was joking, and when I finally did he walked off laughing. Even though he wasn't being serious I couldn't help but think he was a womaniser. Little did I know that he was testing me to see if I was just like all the other women in this industry;

there would be many more tests to come without my realising they were being put in front of me. I was just being me, and because of that I seemed to pass them all.

When Hugh returned to the table I couldn't stop looking at him; I was so confused by my actions, I had completely lost control. I decided that it was best to keep my mouth shut and maintain as much distance as possible. I sat there, willing the minutes to pass so I could finally catch the breath that I had been unconsciously holding.

All night his phone had been ringing but he refused to answer it. When it started to vibrate on the table for the millionth time he apologised and took the call.

'What?' he snapped as his gaze bore straight through me. I felt the heat return to my cheeks, and looked away immediately before exhaling to ease the growing pain in my chest. I took a deep breath in, keeping my focus on the floor, blind to everything around me but the sound of his dark and dangerous voice. I felt cold sweat form on the back of my neck as I heard a woman on the other end of the phone; all the while Hugh's piercing eyes burned into me.

He ended the call tersely, and when I finally regained composure I could see that he was tossing up something in his head. Eventually he lifted his gaze and kept his eyes focused on my boss, speaking directly to her and avoiding my eyes. He said, 'I'm so sorry for what's about to happen. I haven't caught up with a friend in a while and she would like to join us. This could be painful.' Even though he didn't look at me when he spoke I could sense the words were directed at me.

We didn't realise just how painful it would be until I noticed in the mirror a leggy blonde walk in from behind me. He muttered, 'Oh God,' almost inaudibly before getting up to greet her. The woman sat and began to make demands of the surrounding waiters: she wanted something to eat even though the restaurant was closing. I was intrigued by the company he kept, and although I knew I shouldn't I enjoyed feeling the tension in the air between the two of them. All I could think at the time was that my instinct about him—that he was a player—was revealing itself to be true, which made my heart sink but also allowed me to keep a clear head.

Looking at him became easier because he wasn't focused on me as intently, instead concentrating on the conversation he was engaged in with my boss and her husband. Sneaking glances as often as I could without raising suspicion, I was able to observe things about him that I had been blocked from earlier in the night, such as the fact that he wasn't wearing a wedding ring and there was no white band around his finger. I feigned interest in my conversation with the blonde woman—whom I shall nickname 'Pain'—until she caught me off guard by asking me how I had met Hugh. The conversation at the other end of the table stopped and I could feel Hugh's eyes burning into me. I told the story of our phone call and my voicemail message before she told me how lucky I was that he responded because it always took him two weeks to respond to *her* text messages—and they hadn't seen each other in eighteen months. I could tell that she was desperate for his attention, and I stifled a laugh inside that was begging me to let it out.

Clearing his throat, Hugh then spoke up and said that he had received around three hundred messages that day and when he listened to my mine he felt he *had* to call me back; something in my voice had made him want to. The whole table went quiet; I was stunned into silence. At the time I had no idea what this had meant but I could feel the frustration oozing from the woman next to me. I think it was then that she decided she didn't like me. Breaking the silence, Hugh called a waiter over and ordered drinks. He strategically placed a dessert menu in front of us all, and as I reviewed it I silently begged my boss to say she didn't want anything so we could leave and I could escape the frosty looks that Pain was sending my way. Without moving my eyes from the menu I commented to my boss that the strawberry sorbet with custard tart sounded delicious, to which Hugh agreed and smiled at me. I had to force my eyes to stop moving their way up to meet his; it was unnerving how it felt so natural and right.

Pain caught his smile and remarked snidely, 'You like the tarts, don't you, Hughie?' Again the table fell silent. My eyes locked on to him in the moment before he turned to look at her with a disgusted look on his face and said 'No!' Before I had the chance to gasp, she replied, laughing, 'Oh, that's right, you like the *sweet* tarts.'

The conversation from there became extremely uncomfortable, and after dessert we decided to say goodnight. As we got up to leave my boss and her husband walked ahead of me. Pain sauntered straight to the bar without saying goodbye, throwing me one final smirk and wink before sitting down and ordering another drink. I was utterly embarrassed for Hugh but it set his obvious reputation solidly in my mind—he was a serious player. I followed closely behind my boss trying my hardest not to run to the car and lock the doors. Hugh caught up to me and grabbed my arm with such force he spun me towards him until I was an inch from his face. He looked me straight in the eyes and seemed ready to speak but was at a loss as to what to say. There was something in his eyes that showed me he was desperate for me to stay, and it made me want to run. I could feel it emanating from his core; I knew then that this was not the end of something but the beginning. I realised that he hadn't called the meeting merely to discuss business, but whatever else he had in mind, I was determined that it would only ever be in his mind. I didn't know this man but from what I had just witnessed I promised myself I would never be another notch in his belt. I returned his gaze and could not draw my eyes away, until the moment my boss turned to say goodnight and jolted me back to reality.

I broke the connection in an instant, thanked Hugh for his hospitality and walked away without a further word. I reached the car and turned to see him standing in the same spot with his mouth open; I don't know what he had expected but he obviously realised he wasn't going to get it. Moments after we drove off my phone began to beep, bombarded with text messages apologising for what had happened and asking if he could see me again. I was curious to know if my boss or her husband had noticed anything between Hugh and me during the night, but I didn't dare bring it up in case I had completely misread the signs. I hesitated before responding because I knew I was treading on dangerous ground, but something inside me was screaming *yes* so loudly it almost overpowered my logic. Little did I realise at the time that during the meeting Hugh had asked my boss if he could borrow me the following week to attend a national event with him, and she had agreed. No matter what excuses I might try to cook up, my boss had already said yes on my behalf, but that didn't mean I couldn't let him think otherwise.

I texted him back and told him I would think about the event and check my schedule. We ended up exchanging messages until 12.30 a.m. when I finally said goodnight.

What happened the next morning when I woke up was the beginning of something I could not escape. Fate has a way of catching you by surprise, and I certainly wasn't looking for what it had in store for me.

#SecondConfession

#COAMMPlaylist:

'Truly Madly Deeply'

Savage Garden

The morning after that first night, as I was heading out the door I grabbed my phone and saw I had a message from Hugh. I opened it cautiously and saw six words that made my heart skip a beat.

I need to see you again.

I looked at the time stamp and was shocked to see that it had been sent at two that morning. A million things ran through my head at that moment but the most prominent was curiosity. What had happened to Pain? Had she stayed the night with Hugh?

As I stared at my phone, all I could think was that surely this was some kind of sick joke the universe was playing on

26

me. I had not long broken up with a guy who had told me I was too career driven and he was intimidated by my industry, and previous experiences with the wrong type of men had left me insecure and a little scatterbrained. I really couldn't read people—especially men—like I had been able to in the past.

During the trip to the office I tried to think of the best way to reply to Hugh's message but every time I wrote something I ended up deleting it. I really wanted to keep our relationship professional, so I responded by saying that he would need to email me details of the event and I would see if I could make it. Within twenty minutes of hitting send I received a call. I forced myself to remain calm and casual as I answered and graciously declined his invitation to dinner that night. He repeatedly asked me the same question, and again and again I thanked him but said no. Finally he got the message that I wanted to keep things professional, and when I arrived at work thirty minutes later and opened my inbox I found his email waiting, almost taunting me. I looked at my schedule and agreed to go with him.

For the next week he messaged me every day without fail. I couldn't get rid of him. Even though I wasn't interested in him, I can't say that it wasn't flattering. I was, however, confused as I tried to figure out his real motive. I knew from experience that every man had one, and I was determined not to have anything to do with him in any other capacity unless I knew what it was he really wanted.

Throughout the week I stopped myself from posing the question I most wanted to—until, in a moment of weakness during one of our phone calls, I asked him about that night at the restaurant when he had stopped me before I left. What was it he had been going to say to me? His response was unexpected.

'I was going to ask you to stay and have a drink with me. I wanted to be near you, find out more about you. I didn't just want you to stay . . . I needed you to stay. You fascinate me, and you didn't kiss my arse like most people do. I was so confused and intrigued by you from the moment you called, I had to know more about you. I just wanted to be near you . . . your innocence is so refreshing.' I could barely believe my ears. I responded with a 'Thank you' and left it at that.

In all honesty I was floored by his response. I didn't know at the time if it was genuine, but regardless, I wasn't expecting it. He was saying all the right things and yet there was something about him I didn't trust, something that made me hesitant to respond. In the past I had fallen for smooth lines too easily and I was determined not to allow anyone to get close to me again, but suddenly I found myself imagining what it would be like to allow him into a place I thought I had closed off a long time ago. There was simply something about Hugh that made me want to find out more about him.

Over the next two weeks of messaging back and forth I continued to deny him the chance to meet with me, so he started to share more about himself. I was terrified, excited and also wary, and I didn't tell a soul about our exchanges.

•

The more I learned about the entertainment industry the more I found myself not only loving it but thriving on the long hours and lack of sleep. I found that the longer I stayed up working on something, the more I felt I had achieved in my day. When I entered the industry I really had no idea what it was I was getting myself into. I thought that it would be easy to build a reputation, gain new clients and create contacts based solely on hard work. As my determination to become successful in my own right grew daily, I realised that the only way I was going to be able to make a name for myself in the industry was through hard work and a track record of clients with success behind their names.

My first official client was Maria, a musical genius who became an overnight sensation. I focused every waking moment on continuing to build her already successful brand and ensuring that nothing stood in the way of the overall goal of making her a household name across the globe. With her stunning looks and incredible vocals this wasn't too hard; she was a record label's dream. I was determined to do everything I could to make sure her debut album took the world by storm.

Maria was someone who I had admired throughout my teenage years. It is because of her work that I feel a connection with many different genres of music. I remember watching her videos and feeling the buzz as the world became captivated by her beauty and undeniable talent; I watched her go from sitting in her room with nothing but a computer and a video camera to travelling the globe and being hunted by major labels in less than a week, while the media spun her overnight success into a tightly packaged PR stunt. Even then, as a teenager, I felt that I knew better. I could see that she wasn't being very well protected, and after signing a record contract she disappeared online and I stopped watching.

At eighteen I had made the decision to enter into the public relations industry, and when I was allowed to take the company I worked for in a new direction, music was the first sector I wanted to pursue. I knew that it was risky and that there was a lot of competition in the field, but I felt that it was where I was destined to end up.

Boyce Avenue, an American trio who would go on to become an incredibly famous YouTube band, were about to hit the big time and before they did, I contacted their manager and offered to do PR for them in Australia if they were interested in touring here. I was in awe of their talent and would have loved to have been a part of their successful migration into the Australian market. It was all set to go until they decided that they didn't want to tour anytime soon. This was the first time my services had been knocked back, but it didn't deter me at all. I knew what I wanted and, somehow, I was going to get it.

A few days after I received the email from Boyce Avenue, which crushed a little bit of my confidence, I remembered the musician I had followed throughout my teenage years and decided to check up on what she was up to. I was disappointed to discover that in the two years since I had watched her music videos, nothing had really happened. Not only had she seemingly disappeared, but all of a sudden she was no longer signed. I couldn't understand how a major label couldn't have seen her potential to be the next big thing.

This discovery put a fire in my belly, and I was determined to do what the one-directional, tunnel-visioned A&R folks couldn't do. It took me only a few seconds of googling to find the artist's email address, and I fired off my first email to someone who I believed in so strongly that I knew I would be able to secure her as a client without any hesitation. Any disappointment I'd felt about Boyce Avenue vanished, and I felt reinvigorated.

Three months went by in a flash as I became busier than I had ever imagined, putting together events to build up my professional résumé, and I had completely forgotten about the email that I had sent. One morning when I arrived at the office I checked my phone and was surprised to see Maria had left me a voicemail.

To say that I was excited was an understatement. This girl had been an idol for me in my teenage years, and all of a sudden I was faced with the prospect of calling her a client. As soon as I calmed down I tried to call her back, but reached her voicemail. I saw that she had sent me an email and I fired off a response apologising for missing her call.

Later that evening we ended up in a conversation that completely changed the course of my career. I can remember the conversation like it was yesterday. I was flustered at hearing her voice—I couldn't believe that it was really her I was talking to on the other side of the world, let alone the fact that she was calling to discuss the possibility of us working together. It was 7 p.m. and I was energetically pacing up and down the street, while she was on the way to the studio, and I knew my time was limited.

I told her that I had followed her career for some time and was honest enough to tell her what she was doing wrong and how she needed to fix things. The brutally honest approach was risky and might have showed my inexperience, naivety and of course youth, but it also showed that I was enthusiastic and ready to do whatever it took. After twenty minutes of throwing ideas back and forth, she stopped me mid-sentence.

'I'm almost at the studio, Ava. I completely agree with everything you are saying . . .' My heart sank with each word—this was someone that was a *must*-have on my roster of clients. Had I blown it?

'Would you manage my career?' she asked in her songbird voice. All cohesive thoughts vanished from my mind. After talking nonstop for the past twenty minutes I was now lost for words.

'Absolutely. But I've never managed anyone before!'

'You believe in me like no one else ever has. I have faith that you will figure it out.' Hearing those words gave me the confidence to prove her right. The conversation made me realise that as long as I had passion and believed in what I was doing, anything was possible.

It wasn't long before I had a number of clients whose success drew attention to our company as the new kid on the block. We had brands approaching us to work with them, throwing free merchandise not only to the clients but also to the staff in hopes of gaining publicity in any way that they could.

The attention was incredible and a great confidence booster, but I knew that to become as successful as I wanted to be, I needed to build relationships with the people who made the biggest decisions, be they network executives, magazine editors or record label executives. I knew that as long as I had a product that was a must-have, building the relationship would be simple. My biggest problem was the fact that, in reaching for clients I believed in, I had signed up a lot of overseas acts and was now having to learn quickly how the industry worked in other counties. Anyone who knows me knows that I love a challenge, and this is where my motto stems from—'Fake it till you make it'—and that's exactly what I did.

•

The night before the cocktail party I was due to attend with Hugh, he called me to confirm details. He let me know that my father's all-time favourite football player would be attending and I asked if I could bring my dad. Hugh loved the idea, and I felt better knowing I would have back-up.

I was running late for the party, which is very unusual for me, and as my father and I made our way to the venue I was bombarded with text messages and calls from Hugh asking where I was and whether I really was going to go. I kept a level head and promised that I would be there soon.

When we arrived we saw more than a hundred people sitting in the hotel lobby bar at the grandest hotel in the city. I entered wearing my $700 high heels, a black satin top and a pair of killer skinny jeans. My confidence was soaring as I entered what appeared to be a boys' club. I looked around the room and noticed only two other women, both with their cleavage hanging out, who were all over Hugh like a rash.

When I finally reached him I smiled, shook his hand and introduced him to my father. Hugh shook the women off and walked over to introduce my father to his football idol, where he remained for nearly the entire evening locked in conversation, and they ended up getting along like a house on fire.

At one point Hugh attempted to pull me down to sit on his lap but I refused, choosing to remain standing. He was in a super playful mood but I wasn't having any of it. I was there for the sake of my career and I wasn't going to make myself look like a groupie—if that was what he wanted, he could surely have his pick out of the two women opposite me, who were both shooting me daggers. Eventually the chair next to Hugh became empty, and he pulled it closer and asked me to sit with him. I smiled and sat down, feeling a little out of place because I didn't know any of the other guests. Hugh was engaged in conversation with those around him, so I took the opportunity to begin a conversation with a well-known celebrity to my left—we will call him Adam. I had seen him around before, on television and in the press, so I was able to engage with him on an intellectual level. I have always been respected for my intelligence and when I entered the entertainment industry I promised myself that I wouldn't change around someone who had gained a bit of fame. When, after an hour, I began to tell Adam about myself, he looked like he had been smacked in the face. 'So *you're* Ava!' he exclaimed and leaned closer. 'You know he wouldn't shut up about you all fucking day? He kept stressing about when you would get here. I think he was worried you wouldn't show up. I've never seen him like this before. He *really* likes you.'

I froze, struggling to form words in my head, but I eventually managed to respond to Adam with, 'Sure he does,' and laughed it off, presuming Adam had set it up with Hugh.

The entire night Hugh didn't take his eyes off me as I mingled with the people whose company I felt would benefit me the most. I knew I had to be professional, but it was extremely hard when I knew he was only a few feet away at all times. I watched him as closely as he watched me but I was careful not to let him catch me doing so.

Later, as my father and I sat in intense hour-long conversation with a famous footballer who told us about his life before football, I could feel Hugh's eyes boring into me from across the circle of chairs, and my phone started to vibrate.

Hugh repeatedly texted me asking if I was okay and if he could steal me away to talk by the elevators. I responded that I was fine and left it at that; I could handle being in a room with him, surrounded by other people, but the thought of being alone with him and not knowing what to expect, or whether I would be able to hold on to self-control, unnerved me more than I cared to admit.

Soon I realised that Hugh had claimed the empty seat next to me. My hand was on the armrest as I leaned in towards the footballer to hear what he was saying. He was lowering his voice as he talked about his personal life. In a split second my hand lit on fire as I felt Hugh brush his hand over it.

I winced as I felt him grab my hand, squeezing it before he pulled me closer to him and placed my hand on his lap while he drew on my palm with his finger. It was an unexpected delight. It felt so right, but also dangerous, and I was determined not to let him see that I was enjoying it. He continued to text me even though I was sitting right next to him, his messages begging me to walk away so he could talk to me alone. As tempted as I was all I could think was that my father was right next to us. I didn't respond to his messages or the pain bordering on pleasure that was shooting through my arm from his electrifying touch.

After an hour Hugh tapped me on the shoulder. I looked straight into his beautiful, intense brown eyes and felt my breath catch. I found myself scanning his face and imagining what it would be like to kiss him, to feel his lips on mine. It sent a tingle of anticipation through me but I knew I had to snap out of it; he was just so intoxicating. He leaned in closer to whisper in my ear, his breath so silent in the crowded room, but before he had the chance to say anything I looked straight at him as a smile spread across my face and said, 'I know.' It escaped my mouth before I could stop it and I felt so stupid. How could you fall for someone so quickly and yet know nothing about them? I knew it was crazy.

He pulled me closer and whispered, 'I don't care how long it takes, one of these days I'll make you see that I'm good for you. I'm a good person, Ava, and I've never felt like this before . . . and I barely even know you!' My eyes darted in the direction of my father, sitting opposite us and still engrossed in his conversation. It was like Hugh was reading my mind. With that he got up and asked my father if he wanted another drink. I was itching to leave, and a wave of relief washed over me as my father declined and we both agreed to go.

As we said goodbye to Hugh I felt torn: part of me wanted to leave and another part wanted to stay. The look in his eyes promised me that he meant what he had said, but how could I accept that *and* maintain a professional relationship with him? I knew it would be a challenge to fight the feelings that were growing so rapidly inside me, but I have never been one to back down from a fight, and I wasn't about to start.

#ThirdConfession

#COAMMPlaylist
'With You'
Jessica Simpson

The feeling you get right when you start to fall for someone is one of the best things in the world and often sets the tone for what is to come should it make the distance. It's the little things that excite me the most: the private jokes, the long looks and, most of all, the butterflies. As a relationship develops the butterflies don't appear as often and the flirtation becomes a little less intense, and it's easy to question where it's headed. I had some horrific experiences growing up that shattered my faith in men, and these left me unable to feel completely comfortable with any man. Whenever I started to get close to someone my instinct would tell me to escape; in spite of what my heart might want, my head tells me to run as fast as I can, and initially with Hugh I experienced the same panic.

•

Growing up I never knew my biological father, for good reason. To say he wasn't the nicest man is an understatement. He was a psychopath who would stop at nothing to cause harm to my mother and anyone in her life.

I have very few memories of my early childhood, and while there are a few that always make me smile there are many more that shaped the fear of intimacy I still experience from time to time.

When I was about three years old, a man who was a friend of my mother's took advantage of me. I remember so vividly the fear that I felt as he held me on his lap early one morning and began to fondle me. Looking back, I feel disgusted that my body failed to register that what was happening was wrong, while my mind forced me to disassociate. I feel as though my body failed me, which I believe is why I have such a problem with intimacy now—I don't trust that my body can tell the difference between fear and pleasure. It's another reason why I have such a tarnished view of the word 'trust' and what it really means.

My first stepfather, Grant, was incredible to me and treated me just like his own child. However, he and my mother weren't destined to last, which caused irreparable damage to my heart when I realised I would never see the man I called 'Daddy' again. Grant was the first in a succession of good men to leave me, whether by choice or forces beyond anyone's control.

But it was the loss of my late grandfather that shattered my world beyond repair. My grandfather's unconditional love made me feel like I had a place in this world; he understood me when no one else could and he never judged me for being different, but the most important thing about my time with him was that he gave me back a little of the innocence that had been stolen from me at such a young age by men who had failed me. I never really grasped the words 'bowel cancer' or what they meant for him. Being so young, I didn't realise that he was living on borrowed time. Even though I cherish every single memory I have of him, those towards the end are by far the best and the worst memories of my childhood.

I watched the strongest, most beautiful person I had ever known deteriorate in front of my eyes, but never once did he feel sorry for himself. Some days were better than others, and on those days I would spend as much time with him as possible, wanting to make sure that every single moment counted.

As he got worse and the reality set in I could feel my heart breaking—I knew he was going to die, but no one could tell me how soon. When the day came that my mother told me he had passed away my heart shattered into tiny little pieces, I felt as though my soul was drifting from my body and tears began prickling the back of my eyes before they erupted down my cheeks. The man who had saved me from myself, made me feel safe in a head full of confusion and pain and the first person to have broken down my walls, was gone forever. A piece of me was taken when he died. I knew he would look after it, but what I feared the most was not knowing how to pick up the rest of the pieces. That was what set me on the path of self-destruction I was to take for the next few years of my life.

•

The morning after the cocktail party I woke up feeling so confused. I didn't know how I was going to hide what I was beginning to feel in order to maintain a professional relationship and pursue my career. Also, my early experiences had left me afraid of intimacy, and I knew deep down that I couldn't bear the thought of being touched. I was genuinely afraid, although I couldn't articulate even to myself what I was afraid of.

When I arrived at the office the morning after the cocktail party, my phone began to ring: it was Hugh. The moment I saw his name I felt an indescribable rush of emotions. I knew that whatever it was that I was facing with Hugh was not only dangerous for my career but also for my sanity. I couldn't bring myself to believe that a man of his calibre would glance twice at someone like me, but maybe that added to the intrigue.

I answered warily, and his voice filled my soul with chills that rippled from the inside out. I closed my eyes as he said, 'Good morning, babe. Fancy breakfast?'

Inside I was screaming. I knew I wanted to say yes but my mind took charge and I said no.

'I want to see you today,' he argued. 'I promise I'll be professional.'

I sighed. 'I really don't know; I have a lot of work to do.'

'Ava, please come in. I'd like to introduce you to some of my clients,' he pleaded.

As business took charge in my mind I hung up, gathered my bag and headed to Hugh's hotel. The best thing about creating and running a new division for the company was that when I needed to make an executive decision, I was able to do so. I had to answer for any business time that wasn't deemed to have been productive, of course, but I never really had that problem. I was so determined to deliver results that I didn't feel like wasting time, which goes against the common conception of my generation.

The whole way to the hotel I trembled from the inside out, wondering what the hell I was doing. I realised I had been kidding myself to say that I was going to be able to keep this professional. It was becoming painful, as if a devil and an angel were on my shoulders and I was stuck in the middle. I have always been prone to anxiety when it comes to men, but with Hugh I felt as though I was being split in two: I wanted to be the carefree young woman who took risks, but then the smart, strong-willed business figure would pop up and remind me I was playing with fire. What if I did entertain whatever this was and then it turned sour?

When I arrived at the hotel I couldn't see him anywhere but I could see the media everywhere. Seeing so many photographers, reporters and important industry people gathered in the grand foyer made me jump inside. I was so scared of being seen with him because I was determined to be viewed as his business associate, not just yet another woman he was photographed with. Walking through the foyer past all the journalists who would never have looked at me under normal circumstances, it began to hit me just how important this man was. I knew the media was there for Hugh's clients but I also knew that their money shot would be anything that included him. It had been months since he had been snapped and yet here I was, invisible to the awaiting media, about to meet him. I prayed that I would not be forced into the public eye so brutally.

I pulled my iPhone out of my bag and called him, but he didn't answer. I called again, part of me aching to hear his voice but another part of me dreading it. When the call again went to voicemail I grew annoyed—after all, he was the one who had begged me to meet with him, had texted me the entire time I was on my way. The media frenzy was causing my anxiety to fly through the roof, adding to my rising impatience, and I turned around and made my way towards the front doors. As I was about to step out into the street I saw one of the women who had been all over Hugh at the event the night before. I stopped dead in my tracks, and then changed my course and walked up to her. I asked if she had heard from Hugh. She recognised me immediately, looked me up and down before saying no but then she whipped out her phone and dialled his number—and he answered straightaway. I can't say that I wasn't confused or a little jealous when he answered her call, and then even more annoyed when I heard her say, 'Hugh, your girlfriend's at reception.'

I immediately felt my face light up, my cheeks burning as I caught sight of my red face in the mirror behind the reception desk. The lump in my throat was harder than ever as I struggled to swallow. I had no idea how to react to this and yet I couldn't bring myself to correct her. I was about to speak when my phone rang.

'Are you going to answer that?' she snapped.

I felt myself float back down to reality and realised that it was Hugh.

'Hey, beautiful. I've told reception to leave you a key, so come up. I'm packing to leave,' he said with a smile in his voice.

'I'll just wait downstairs for you,' I replied in an instant reflex to the knot forming in my stomach.

'No. I'm going to be a while, get the key and come up. I'll introduce you to everyone when I'm finished, but I don't want you to have to wait.' He hung up before I had the chance to respond.

I was tempted to just wait downstairs and risk the media attention because what I feared more than being caught out publicly was being alone in a room with him . . . well, with any man, really. What I realised in an instant was that I barely knew Hugh and even though I felt a level of comfort in his presence I also felt a surge of panic at the thought of being trapped behind closed doors with him. Thinking rationally about my fears, I had to acknowledge that I wasn't sure I would be able to resist his advances.

When I turned around the woman was gone, so I steadied myself and made my way to the concierge, who listened to my name and then immediately treated me like royalty. The hotel manager came straight over and gave me my key card in person.

'Enjoy your stay, Ms Reilly,' he said with a smile and slight bow. 'Mr Montgomery is a very valuable client, so if there is anything you need please contact me directly, any time, day or night.' Not wanting to give him the wrong impression I began to tell him I wouldn't be staying, but I stopped when a staff member appeared from a well-hidden back room and said, 'Mr Montgomery is expecting you.'

This had to be one of the most embarrassing moments of my life. I was so blind to the world around me and could only follow silently as the hotel manager walked me to the elevators and pressed the button for the twenty-third floor.

I stepped into the elevator apprehensively, fiddling with the ring on my finger as the doors closed and the elevator swiftly moved me closer and closer to Hugh. My heart began to pound in my ears and my throat became dry; I was so nervous I couldn't swallow.

The doors opened and I just stood there, unable to move. I felt sick and I didn't want to be there—I wanted to run as far and as fast as I could. Instead, my heart took a step forward and my feet followed.

I walked towards the door of the suite and, forgetting I had the key, I knocked. Moments later Hugh opened the door, dressed casually in a pair of Calvin Klein jeans and an unbuttoned baby-blue business shirt revealing his tanned skin. As he leaned in to kiss my cheek I drank in the smell of his cologne, something from that moment I would always connect with him. I couldn't put my finger on it but something—the freshness of his crisp business shirt or maybe the cologne—began to drive me crazy. I felt a wave of desire wash over me. I forced myself to pull away and walked into the room, clutching my bag so tightly that the buckle started to cut into me.

As I walked in he pulled me close and kissed me again on the cheek, ramping up my desire from a low flame to a roaring fire as I was hit with his intoxicating smell again. He guided me into the suite with his hand on the small of my back, the electricity in his touch shooting through my spine so violently that I jumped forward to get away from his hand. With every touch I could feel the invisible connection between us growing.

I placed my bag on the floor near a chair and looked around the suite in awe. The view of the city was incredible. I walked straight towards the window and, despite my fear of heights, looked down at the little people below going about their daily routines, completely oblivious to the figure standing at the window above them. As I watched them I prayed that I wasn't making a terrible decision; I knew I was playing with fire but I couldn't stop myself. I was quickly becoming addicted to the magnetic pull I felt around him.

Dragging my gaze away from the window and back to the reality in front of me, I looked around the suite: television on, open suitcases, business suits neatly stacked on top of each other on the bed and things everywhere. A wave of relief flooded through me as I saw that Hugh was indeed packing; it hadn't just been a ploy to get me up to his room. I turned my attention back to the window and once again got lost in the sights. Within moments I sensed him standing right behind me, so close that I could feel his body pressed to mine. I instinctively moved my head to the left. The warmth of his breath on my neck sent delightful tingles down my spine, and the electrifying touch of his fingers running down my bare arm gave me goose bumps.

I stood for a second, fighting the urge to turn around and look at him, then reality kicked in and I moved away. He seemed to sense how nervous I was and didn't push it, instead returning to his packing and offering me a cup of coffee. I declined in a small voice, barely able to breathe. Long minutes passed in silence as I sat in an armchair and pretended to focus on the television while he continued to pack suits.

Out of the corner of my eye I saw him drop something in his suitcase and then walk towards me. I felt like everything was in slow motion as I looked straight into his deep dark-brown eyes. I saw the hunger there, and I felt the electricity in the air and my heart stopped as he leaned down and placed the palm of his hand over my jaw, and before I knew it he was kissing me. It was like an explosion of fear, nerves, pain, happiness, butterflies, pure passion and desire as his lips pressed on mine and his tongue explored my mouth with intense yearning. My eyes were closed, amplifying the feelings as I felt a smile spread across his face. He continued to kiss me in the same rushed passion until my right hand reached up and pushed against his chest, forcing him to take a step back.

As my hand dropped he grabbed it, pulled me out of the chair and placed his hand around my waist and in an instant he tried to kiss me again. This time I wasn't going to cave in. I ducked out under his free arm and he spun me around with a hard grasp of my hand and tried once more to kiss me. It was as though we were dancing a familiar dance that I had never learned the steps to; it felt so safe and yet dangerous. I moved my head to the right and he caught my neck, nuzzling into the small crevice between my neck and my shoulder. I allowed myself to close my eyes and drink in the moment before I took a step back.

Before I knew it I was yelling at him. 'Why did you have to go and do that?!'

He looked at me, his normally warm eyes overtaken by a deep, dark, cold stare that made me want to close the gap between us and melt into his arms. I regretted the words instantly; I knew it wasn't right but I wanted to be back in that moment.

'I could see how nervous you were and all I wanted to do was make you more comfortable,' he said. 'I've been dying to kiss you since I met you that first night—and I'm not going to apologise for it!'

Before I had the chance to respond, his phone rang. He didn't move his gaze from me, nor did he budge an inch. Eventually I said, 'Well, aren't you going to get that?'

He looked at me intensely, before snatching his phone from the table and yelling, 'What?' to the innocent person on the other end of the phone, still not taking his eyes off me.

As he spoke I grabbed my bag, and with it I felt instantly protected.

He hung up the phone, and finished packing in silence. Before I knew it we were in the elevator heading down to the foyer, and neither of us had said a word. Something had shifted between us. I hadn't wanted to piss him off but I knew that if I hadn't taken control of the situation I would have lost myself in his presence. I needed to try to pull things back on to a professional level, even though it was killing me inside.

We barely spoke two words to each other except for when he introduced me to his clients. I could feel his fury, but no one else seemed to notice it.

When I left him I felt as though I had screwed everything up. I didn't know if I was ever going to hear from him again and it scared me more than I cared to admit. I cried the entire way back to the office, unable to believe what had happened—I felt like I had destroyed everything, and the thing that confused me the most was that I couldn't understand why it hurt so much.

#FourthConfession

#COAMMPlaylist:

'It Must Have Been Love'

Roxette

While I continued to fight my growing feelings for Hugh I also knew that it was only a matter of time until I was consumed by them. One question burned in my mind: had I lost my chance?

The night after my hotel tousle with Hugh I sat in my bedroom, trying to stop myself from contacting him. I couldn't help but play with my phone; I wanted to send him a message even though I knew I shouldn't. I couldn't bear it if he told me he never wanted to see me again but at the same time I had to know. I felt so lost and caught up in feelings I had never intended to feel—it was nothing short of excruciating. I was not entirely sure why I was fighting with myself—I had never been the type of person to shy away from my feelings, but for some reason this was different; I was completely frozen at even the thought of him.

It took me two hours before I finally wrote a message that I didn't delete: *I really want to be able to keep this professional but you are making it so hard for me.* Once I hit send I threw my phone across the bed; I didn't want it anywhere near me, as I was petrified of his response—good, bad or indifferent. I think that instinctively I knew I was on the path of no return, no matter how hard I tried to fight it.

The whole night I tortured myself, desperate to hear back from him but also scared of what he would say. As the hours wore on, that fear turned to anger: *he* had been constantly messaging me and now he wouldn't respond to *me*. I knew this was irrational, but that made no difference. I think I just needed some reassurance that it wasn't all in my head. I fell asleep with tears rolling down my cheeks, convinced I had lost my chance.

Two days passed and I decided to force Hugh from my mind. It was incredibly hard but I had to do it; obviously he had nothing left to say, and I wasn't about to become Pain #2.

The next morning as I stepped out of the shower I saw two missed calls on my phone from Hugh and a message waiting. My heart jumped into my throat, and my palms began to sweat as I fumbled with my phone, trying to unlock it.

I'm sorry, I dropped my phone in a bucket of water the other night and have only just got everyone's numbers back. Tried to call you. Call you in a while. x

I needed to hear his voice and to know if he was still angry with me, so I immediately tried to call him back, but he didn't answer. For the next few hours my phone was glued to my hand.

When he eventually called I trembled as I answered. I wasn't sure what I wanted to say and I had no idea the type of mood he would be in; it wasn't as if we had left things on good terms. I was on the verge of begging for forgiveness and yet I still couldn't tell him why I reacted the way I did, why I couldn't let him touch me.

•

All the pain in my childhood culminated in me heading down the path of self-destruction. My first stepfather leaving, not knowing the full truth about my biological father, the sexual abuse and my grandfather's passing had taken their toll on me, and I was full of mixed emotions that I was not equipped to handle. All the negative experiences in my life had collided together and blocked me from making any decision that was rational or even sane. I had been suspended from school numerous times, had caused heartache and pain for anyone who came into contact with me, and even though I was suffering I would never let anyone close enough to find out why.

With the help of a very persistent teacher I was just beginning to get my life back on track when the next shattering experience occurred to completely destroy my trust in men.

I was almost sixteen when I came down with a severe case of the flu and my parents asked my step-grandfather to look after me. My nan was at work and although I wasn't close to my step-grandfather I thought that he would look after me through my sickness.

I was too sick to do much and was incredibly bored, sitting at the computer talking to my aunt on instant messaging while my step-grandfather sat at the dining room table, drinking his millionth beer for the morning. It was obvious that he was drunk, but I knew that if I steered clear of him he wouldn't try to teach me to fight again like he had so many times before. His way of teaching always left me feeling a little off as I would inevitably end up pinned to the ground when he won and he would lay on top of me with his hands pressed firmly to my wrists, laughing and taunting me as I struggled to get out of his grip.

As I sat at the computer I began to get frustrated at being exhausted and aching all over. I began to cry, which only intensified the aching, and soon I felt like I might pass out from the pain.

He got up from the dining table and walked over to me and then tried to massage my shoulders. Alarm bells went off in my head at his touch, telling me to get away and scream at him to stop, but the pain that wracked my body made me ignore my instincts. I tried to push my fears to the back of my mind and act rationally.

The massage was beginning to help until I felt his hand run down the left side of my shirt and grab my breast. Gathering my willpower, I moved my arm up to stop him, but he tightened his grip and the feeling of dread spread through me so rapidly that I thought I was going to be sick. I begged him to stop but I could hear his sadistic, drunken smile in his voice as he spoke.

'Why? No one will know.'

I was terrified of the consequences of standing up to him, but I could feel the bile rising in my throat and I couldn't stand it any longer.

'*I* will!' I yelled, shoving his hand away from me with as much force as I could muster. I held in my tears and tried to wish it all away. I felt violated once again, and I couldn't understand what I had done to deserve this treatment twice in one lifetime.

I will never forget the way that he yelled at me after I denied him his perverted wish. I felt disgusted at myself for everything that these men had done to me, and because of my recent self-destructive behaviour I knew that I couldn't tell anyone about this. Not only would it ruin my family, but I was afraid that my parents and nan wouldn't believe me.

I managed to take myself to the spare bedroom and sat there pleading with myself to try to stay awake and not pass out while I was alone in the house with him. I rang my aunt and told her what had happened and made her promise not to tell anyone, because no one would ever believe me with my recent bad behaviour. She argued and begged me to tell my parents, but I just didn't want people to be disgusted in me. I couldn't handle the feeling that it was my fault. Obviously I had done something to deserve this happening again. An hour later he entered the room and sat next to me on the bed. I instinctively pulled my knees up to my chest as he looked directly at me.

'Who did you tell?' He had overheard me on the phone.

I said I hadn't told anyone, but he didn't believe me, which heightened my fear, even though I had been on high alert ever since he had come into the room.

He asked me the question again and I responded with the same answer, but I felt the wooziness start to overtake my body. I focused desperately on staying awake, afraid of what might happen next, but even more afraid of losing control. The feeling of disassociation I had felt when I had been abused when I was younger seemed more terrifying than whatever he might do to me.

Before I knew what was happening he turned around to face me, and then hugged me. I froze. I was in no state to push him away—all of my remaining strength was concentrated on staying in control of my state of mind. I knew I was losing the battle, and I prayed to my grandfather in heaven to help me. I couldn't see any way that I was going to get out of this unscathed.

He finally pulled away and whispered words that made me feel violated all over again.

'Good. Let's keep it our little secret,' he said, and then walked out of the room, leaving me shellshocked and unsure of how I was going to handle this on my own, because telling my family, apart from my aunt, was out of the question.

In the months that followed I managed to keep up appearances, but inside I was destroyed. My behaviour ended up deteriorating until I was expelled from school, but by that stage I really didn't care. I was sick and tired of my life, and could no longer pretend to care about what was going to happen to me next.

There was nothing that anyone could have done at the time to help me. I was a master of masking my pain, and the only outward sign that something was wrong was that I was acting out more than usual. To anyone looking on, it just seemed like an escalation of my recent bad behaviour.

Eventually I reached my breaking point when my step-grandfather king-hit me in the face after I had had an argument with my nan. The white, blinding pain was something I will never forget, and it awoke a rage inside that surprised even me.

I told my nan everything through a torrent of angry tears and she sat there too stunned to speak. This was exactly the reaction I had expected from her and he stood there listening to my admission, never once denying it but instead resorting to childish name-calling.

My mother's reaction, however, is the one that sticks with me most vividly, and although I now understand that she reacted in shock, I still feel as though she blamed me for what had happened, and it broke me even further.

'Well if he didn't touch me when I was younger, and I walked around in bikinis, why should I believe he touched you?'

I felt abandoned by my family, and this was exactly why I hadn't wanted to tell anyone in the first place. I knew I was going to end up living with the pain of this experience for the rest of my life. My trust in other people, especially men, was gone and I knew that I would never be able to allow a man to touch me without the memories and feelings of dread consuming me. From that point on I felt totally out of control in intimate situations, and because of that I vowed to never let anyone breach the walls I had built up to protect myself, lest they take the only piece of my sanity that was left.

•

I couldn't bring myself to tell anyone about the memories that had haunted me over the past few years; I didn't even want to admit to myself that it had happened. But before I could speak, Hugh did.

'Ava,' he said gently, 'I don't know what's going on with you, but I'm sorry. I promise you, I will never push your boundaries. I promise I will never hurt you.' My heart fluttered with each syllable and a wave of relief washed over me. In the instant that I heard his voice I had flashbacks of the feeling he had aroused in me as he stood behind me in that hotel room, when he whipped me around to face him, strong and forceful, and yet gentle and kind.

My next few words slipped out before I could stop them. 'When are you going to be in town next?' I breathed.

'I'll be back in two weeks, and I want to see you. No work, no interruptions. Just us.'

I immediately accepted; I wasn't going to make the same mistake twice. I felt so blissfully happy in that moment, knowing that my past was not going to ruin something I didn't even know I wanted.

Over the next two weeks we messaged back and forth and spoke at least twice a day. My feelings grew and yet he was a closed book; I had known that from the moment we met but I had no idea just how closely he guarded his privacy. He gave me small insights into his lifestyle, he was funny, charismatic and down to earth, yet I couldn't figure out how he really felt about me.

On the Friday I was to meet him at the hotel, those horrible feelings of insecurity came back, and suddenly I wanted to run. When it came to business, I felt in control and never had a problem, but when it came to sorting out my personal life I just didn't know where to start.

As I walked through the hotel lobby I felt like all eyes were on me. A shiver ran down my spine: I wanted to be there but I was frightened of what might happen and what it might mean. I stepped into the elevator and went straight up to the bar. As I sat with a glass of wine, Hugh called from the airport, apologising profusely because he was stuck on the tarmac and would be twenty minutes late. Although this made me breathe easier because it gave me time to compose myself, it also made it harder to think clearly because no matter how long it took him to get there I would still have to face him. A voice inside my head told me to leave, but I took a deep breath and decided to stay.

I ordered Hugh a drink; I always made an effort to pay attention to the little things, so I knew his choice of drink and the specific way he liked it served. I sipped my wine and chose a table from where we could watch the football match. I wasn't a big fan but I knew he was, and I figured that if he was distracted it might give me the chance to read him a little better and figure out what it was about him that had me so captivated.

Exactly twenty minutes later, Hugh arrived. I sensed him before he even came around the corner. I felt a shift in the atmosphere and with shaky hands placed my drink on the table before I turned my head to the left and I saw him coming up behind me.

As I stood up and smoothed down my dress, my senses were in overdrive. The familiar tingle of his touch coursed through me as his fingertips rested on my hand. I struggled to breathe through the intense feelings clouding my body and soul as he leaned down and placed a gentle kiss on my cheek.

He sat opposite me, facing away from the television. I leaned over the coffee table and pushed his drink towards him. He downed it in one gulp, and I could feel that his nerves were just as strong as mine. When he finished he asked me to wait for him while he checked in and put his bags in his room.

'Would you like another drink?' I asked calmly, trying to hide my own nerves and hoping he would say yes so I would have an excuse to get myself another glass of wine.

'Yes, please,' he responded as he began to pull out his card.

'Don't be stupid,' I said. 'I'm not taking your money. I'll get it.' I tried to hide the fact that the sight of his card—and his assumption that I would expect him to pay—offended me a little.

'Ava, did you charge the drinks to my room?' he asked calmly. *Now* I was offended. What type of woman did he take me for?

'Of course not!' I said hotly. Obviously he thought I was just after his money, but I never even bothered to think about how much he was actually worth.

'I'm not taking it,' I responded as he waved his card in the air. I refused to even look at it.

He watched me, as if he was testing me, but I wasn't going to cave in. The thought of taking money from him was cheapening; I liked to earn my money and would not accept it from some guy who obviously gave it so freely.

He continued to watch me but didn't put his card away, so I lowered my voice as I said to him, 'I'm not going to take your fucking money. I have my own and I can certainly pay for a drink. Stop trying to control everything.' It slipped out before I had the chance to stop myself. I sat there a little shocked that I had actually had the guts to say it. He didn't look surprised at all, though; in fact the look on his face told me he had enjoyed it. His calmness infuriated me.

He placed his hand on my leg and rubbed his thumb across my kneecap while giving me a beautiful smile. A cold shiver erupted from my core in reaction to his touch as the insecurities buried just beneath the surface began to rise; my knee jolted violently to the left, away from his electrifying touch, and hit the coffee table. The pain was excruciating, but I tried to hide it, hoping he hadn't noticed. But it was too late.

'What, am I not allowed to touch you?' he said. 'Seriously, Ava, you are so wound up, you need a good fuck to loosen you up. I've never met someone so uptight and jumpy. I was just trying to show you that everything's okay between us.' His tone was soothing yet ferocious.

His words were like music to my soul even though I was confused. The only solace I took from his statement was that we were okay . . . whatever that meant. I found myself easing into a comfortable place where I was able to relax a little, and I think he sensed this.

He left me to go and unpack and I ordered our next drinks. I could tell that he wasn't happy that I had won our disagreement, but surely I wasn't the first person to have told him no. My heart pounded the entire time he was gone, and once again I could sense him and smell his cologne before he returned behind me.

When he sat back on the long couch opposite me I couldn't look him in the eye. I clasped my drink hard as I felt his gaze pierce into me. He had one arm stretched out to the right of him on the back of the couch and the other held the drink he sipped slowly as he watched me. I was so self-conscious. I knew he was trying to read me like I ws trying to read him but I didn't want him seeing right through me, so I drank faster. Almost immediately I started to feel the alcohol take effect as my mind became fuzzy. My inhibitions were lowering and I knew I had to escape or there would be no turning back.

We barely spoke during the rest of our time together; he just watched me, which was very unnerving. I tried to distract him with the football game on the television behind him but it didn't work; he barely glanced at it before he turned back to me again. I couldn't help but steal a look at his wedding ring finger and again I noticed it was bare. I knew he had been married once, and I was curious as to why he hadn't been again.

'So, why is it that you didn't remarry?' The words had left my mouth before I realised how intrusive they could be. Finishing my sentence, I was a little concerned that he would take offence and once again I would be back at square one with him. I could feel his eyes burning into me as I took another sip of my drink. I had no idea how he was going to react. It felt like an eternity before he spoke again.

'Ava, I'm not divorced. I couldn't see myself dating young women anyway, they get too clingy and it's really not worth the headache,' he said so casually that I almost choked on my wine. A million things ran through my mind as sweat began to gather on the back of my neck. I felt my core turn to stone and in an instant I felt myself retreating to the safety of my shell. What the hell did that mean?

The room filled with silence again as I tried to comprehend why he had been so forward with information that I hadn't even asked for. I wished I'd never asked such a thoughtless question. I vacillated between being desperate to find out exactly what he meant by 'not divorced', trying to think of subtle ways to change the conversation and wishing the ground would open up and swallow me whole to get me out of the situation I'd created. I looked around and saw the barmen cleaning glasses. I kept my eyes on them as my mind ran a mile a minute but my mouth couldn't catch up to ask more questions.

Eventually he broke the silence. 'Well?'

I shot daggers at him and said, 'Well . . . I have to go. It was lovely seeing you again, Hugh.' I placed my drink on the coffee table in front of us, grabbed my bag and rose to leave. His jaw dropped and his eyes widened before he downed his drink and he placed it so hard on the table the sound vibrated through the room. He jumped up and followed me to the elevator in stunned silence. He didn't need to touch me for me to feel the heat blazing from his skin. He was so close, I could feel his presence behind me.

We entered the elevator as 'Un-Break My Heart' by Tony Braxton played. As soon as the doors closed he cornered me. I had nowhere I could escape to as my fears rose to the surface, my heart racing so much I thought I would faint. I looked around frantically for the emergency button and realised it was behind me; I was trapped in the corner with the metal bar digging into my hip and couldn't reach the button, which only caused me further stress. I felt tears pricking my eyes, threatening to explode as he took me by force with his fingers digging into my skin, his hands holding on to my arms for dear life. He pushed me harder against the bar and kissed me. The sheer force of passion in his kiss froze me to the spot and he wouldn't let me go. He pushed himself closer to me and I felt every contour of his body melding into mine: a perfect fit. I couldn't kiss him back, I couldn't breathe, I couldn't do anything. Within me lust and passion battled a fear that I had never experienced before.

The doors parted slowly as I opened my eyes and pulled away, gasping for air. He stepped back and just looked at me. I could see his chest rise and fall with each breath he took.

I was so close to pushing every button in that elevator to resume the moment of passion I had just experienced, but I couldn't—I knew if I did, I would regret it in the morning. I didn't know what he had meant about not being divorced, and being with a married man went against everything I had ever believed in. Even if he wasn't with her, they were still married. I was not about to become the other woman.

I picked up my bag from the floor—I hadn't even realised it had fallen from my shoulder—and refused to look at him as I walked out into the wide space of the lobby just as the doors began to close. My eyes were filled with tears again, and I heard him say 'Fuck' as he watched me walk away. When I reached the glass doors I slowly turned around to take one last look at the man I knew I had to say goodbye to. I was not about to get involved with a married man . . . no matter what it cost me in the short term, I knew the long-term consequences would be even more devastating.

#FifthConfession

'A Case of You'

Javier Colon

On the way home that night I was a shambles. I was so scared of what I was feeling, and I couldn't believe what I was thinking: I still wanted to see him. The hardest thing for me to accept was the fact that despite my mind telling me no—Hugh was a married man—I still wanted to be with him. What rational person would enter into something with a man who could never really be yours and yours alone?

The fear of intimacy and the struggle to keep things professional seemed to dull with distance between us, and a new fear emerged. I was at war with my morals and the feelings I couldn't stop. I didn't have the courage to ask him what 'not divorced' meant—if I heard the dreaded words 'I'm still with her', I wasn't sure I would be able to continue the fight within myself—so I decided I didn't want to know.

On the way home my phone wouldn't stop ringing. I couldn't bring myself to answer it, and after what seemed like forever he finally stopped. Then came the text that I couldn't avoid opening. I fumbled with my phone and opened the message.

Ava, I don't know what more to say. I don't like talking about my life, I don't like texting and I don't like emails. They have been used against me in the past but considering you won't answer my calls and let me explain I have to tell you this way. I have been separated for eighteen months. Stop running away from me and pick up the fucking phone!!!

I read and re-read his message, afraid I was falling into a trap. Had my secret wishes been answered? Was he telling me the truth?

I responded in a cool, calm and collected manner, which was far from what I was really feeling.

Thank you for clarifying this, Hugh. I'm not running from you. I need you to know that I will not be a one-night stand, and if you're looking for that then we may as well just part ways here. I will not lower my standards.

I exhaled slowly as I pressed send. There . . . I had found the courage to say what was in my heart.

He responded moments later: *I wouldn't expect anything less. Call me.*

I didn't call him. I was emotionally exhausted and as soon as I got home I crashed, doing my best to put him out of my mind.

The following morning when I woke up the first thing I did was listen to music to block out my thoughts. I put my iPhone on shuffle and told myself that the next song was going to explain how I felt about the situation with Hugh; that song turned out to be 'Chains' by Tina Arena. I will never forget the memories that this song holds for me; the lyrics express every thought from that time in my life.

I called Hugh on my way to work and he convinced me to meet with him at his beachside apartment that Friday night after he flew into town for meetings. I was apprehensive; I knew that I was considering doing something morally repugnant but even at the sound of his voice I found myself becoming instantly submissive. I kept asking myself what it was that I really wanted and if I was strong enough to endure what would surely be a bumpy road . . . but I always came up blank.

I had agreed to meet him, but only if I brought a friend with me. My biggest fear at that point felt as though it was close to coming true. Despite all of the abuse I had endured in my early childhood I had maintained the only innocence that I could; I was still a virgin, and the idea of sleeping with Hugh left me wondering what the consequences would be for my emotional wellbeing.

After a hectic Friday morning filled with meetings and conference calls, none of which I could concentrate on, I grabbed my bags and made my way to the offices where my friend Leah worked. I had confided in her about everything that had happened between Hugh and me, and she agreed to come with me to make sure I didn't do anything I would end up regretting. That night as we drove out of the city to meet him at his apartment he constantly texted me to confirm we were coming. I could tell he was nervous, but he couldn't have been more nervous than I was.

My heart was racing as we drove along the coast. I knew from the moment I had agreed to meet him that I would end up staying the night with him, but even as we arrived I wasn't sure it was what I really wanted. I wanted to turn back and run away from whatever I was about to face but I knew it was too late.

We pulled into the driveway and I saw him waiting. I swallowed hard as he opened the car door, and I didn't dare to look at him as I stepped out in my newly acquired white Swarovski crystal–encrusted stilettos. As my feet hit the ground I knew I had to feign confidence even though my insides were churning. In my head 'Can't Hold Us Down' by Christina Aguilera played, which gave me the extra edge I desperately needed. I was going to ensure that I had an amazing night . . . with or without Hugh.

I let him kiss me on the cheek but wouldn't let him touch me, afraid that my front would crumble in an instant if I felt even the slightest hint of electricity coursing through my veins. I could feel an icy chill coming from Leah as he hugged her in greeting; I knew she thought he was only after one thing from me.

We walked through the empty foyer and into the elevator before Hugh tried to strike up a conversation. It wasn't as difficult for me to talk to him this time, but I kept my guard up. I knew I needed to loosen up a little but I also needed to keep a level head, so I planned to limit my alcohol consumption. All the while, amid these sensible thoughts, my heart was screaming out that I wanted him now more than ever. I could feel him next to me and the smell of his seductive cologne made it hard to control myself. He seemed so calm and relaxed now compared to me; it made me wonder how many times he had done this before. I immediately felt sick at the thought and tried to push the images of him with other women to the back of my mind as the elevator doors slid open.

When we walked into the apartment I waltzed straight into the master bedroom and placed my bags on the floor. I turned around to see Hugh looking at me, his eyes begging to speak to me alone, but I grabbed Leah by the arm and went to look around the apartment. As we reached the balcony we walked out to see the beach right in front of us, making us gasp in awe. Right next to the ocean was a buzzing city boasting bright lights and a nightlife that was going off even though it was only 7 p.m.

Hugh joined us on the balcony and offered us a drink. Suddenly I wanted to hit the alcohol hard despite my head telling me not to. Now that I was here, with him, I no longer cared—I was going to get blind drunk and I was going to drive him crazy. Leah and I accepted a vodka and lemonade as we sat down and lit up cigarettes. Hugh returned from the kitchen shortly after with an ashtray and said, 'I don't mind you girls smoking but I don't want you to be smoking all night.' I gave him a frosty look and he immediately returned it with a hard stare, as if begging me to try him. I knew I couldn't stare him down for long, but before I broke he backed down and asked where we would like to go for dinner. Neither Leah nor I knew the area well, so Hugh made the decision for us and a little while later we walked downstairs and ended up at an incredible Italian restaurant less than a block from the apartment.

As soon as we walked in, the owner came up to greet Hugh, and we were shown to a table. It was obvious that the staff knew and respected Hugh, and he carried himself through it impressively. He didn't command the attention, it just came naturally to him.

It didn't take long for Leah to warm to Hugh's natural charm, and they began to laugh together. It made things so much easier as we ordered and settled in for an easy, laidback night. I felt like I would finally be able to breathe easily—until a group of women walked in, and one of them marched up to the table and, ignoring Leah and me, addressed Hugh.

'Hugh? Oh my god, I knew it was you! I said to my friend when I walked in that I thought I could smell your cologne!' I dropped my fork on the plate with a loud clatter and it almost fell off the table. Hugh didn't look at me but immediately grabbed my free hand and squeezed it. The tall, leggy brunette in a short white dress with a tan the wrong side of orange said to her friend, 'I bet you he has a bottle on him right now. Can I have some? I love the smell!' I tried to pull my hand away but he held on as I felt my anger build.

Hugh produced the offending object and gave it to her without so much as a smile. He looked at me out of the corner of his eye as she began to spray it on herself and her friend, and I was sure he could feel my fury flowing in her direction. He squeezed my hand but I was too pissed off to care. It took everything I had in me to not say something to this woman who was flirting so outrageously.

It was only when he moved his chair closer to me that she realised he did not want to talk to her. She continued to ignore Leah and me, focusing her attention on him. I tried to yank my hand away from Hugh again as he introduced us but he held on and tightened his grip further. She looked at me in disgust and leaned down to hug him, showing her set of fake assets. I was now well and truly sick of being polite as she threw herself all over him but I knew I really didn't have the right to say anything.

She made a point of telling him she had broken up with her fiancé and would *love* to catch up with him again, before laughing aloud as she waltzed off to her table. The only thought running through my head was that they had obviously slept together at some point. Hugh had promised to call her with no enthusiasm but it didn't ease my frustration.

Leah looked down at her food and Hugh threw me an apologetic smile, clearly sensing that it was best to stay quiet.

After dinner we made our way outside to the car Hugh had arranged to pick us up: a black Hummer. By this point I was well and truly tipsy and lost my footing on the kerb, but fortunately Hugh caught me just before I hit my head on the concrete. I was a nervous wreck and his little friend at the restaurant had only made things worse.

Twenty minutes later we arrived at a nightclub, and as soon as we stepped out of the Hummer I made a point of lighting up a cigarette. I watched as a disappointed look flooded his face but I didn't care, I took one puff and flicked it into the nearby tray before blowing rings. He knew not to press me on this after what had just happened. I have to admit that at this point the alcohol was lowering my inhibitions a little . . . well, maybe a lot.

When we walked into the bar—Hugh leading me by the hand while Leah marched on up ahead—we were immediately escorted to the VIP lounge. When I sat down the manager came to greet Hugh, who sat next to me and refused to let go of my hand. I was incredibly confused, about so many things, especially the giant elephant in the room: his wife. I still didn't know the details of his situation and I was afraid to ask. I found myself wanting to push him away and pull him closer at the same time, which is lethal on its own but throw in alcohol and there was no chance of roping it in and staying in control.

As the manager went downstairs to get us all drinks a group of girls walked up the stairs in tiny dresses, which instantly threw me back to the incident at the restaurant. I could feel the effects of the alcohol taking their toll on me as I felt a sudden rush of irrational jealousy and nervousness infused with confidence, something that was way out of character for me. I leaned over and began to whisper in his ear, making sure I was close enough for only him to hear, but before I got the chance to say a word he pulled back and looked me dead in the eyes as a smile crept across his face and he mouthed one word: 'Behave.' This drove me insane—I wasn't going to jump just because he said to. Ignoring his instruction, I slipped my hand up from his knee, gilding up his thigh, excited about reaching my final destination to drive him as crazy as he was driving me—but before I got the chance he snatched my hand away and looked into my eyes as he kissed my knuckles one by one, then squeezed my hand lightly and placed our entwined hands between us. Just in time, it seemed, because the manager arrived in front of us a minute later and would surely have caught us.

As my drink was placed in front of me I sat silently, not breathing, not moving, but rather knocked for six by his display of controlled intimacy. He could have played along with it, grabbed one of the pillows and let me go to town on him without anyone suspecting a thing, but instead he did the gentlemanly thing and said no. I was blown away; had I found a diamond in the rough?

By the time we made our way out to the car an hour later Leah and Hugh had become instant friends. I put it down to her being absolutely inebriated, but I was just happy that they were finally getting along and I didn't feel like I had to keep an eye on them. As we arrived at our next destination I jumped out of the car with a newfound excitement for the night ahead. I stepped out on to the footpath and was floored the moment I realised where we were . . . a gentlemen's club!

I had never been to anything like it before, but the golden sign above us promised an evening full of excitement. The line to enter trailed around the block, but just like at the previous bar Hugh was greeted immediately, this time by a tall, dark and handsome man with the look of a professional wrestler, a clear cord concealing an earpiece. The guy hugged Hugh as if they hadn't seen each other in years before we were escorted past the queued patrons and up the stairs. Walking ahead of Hugh I could feel his eyes on me; he was so close I could feel his breath on my neck. Tall-dark-and-handsome took us upstairs to the VIP section, where the music pumped all around us and I felt my pulse race with excitement; it was almost as if I knew I shouldn't be there but I was going to enjoy it anyway. I was intrigued by everything that was going on around me, especially the women performing: they were immaculately dressed in full-length gowns and runway-model make-up. I was astounded at how polished they looked.

As the hundreds of patrons watched the live show, the woman performing climbed a pole with expert precision before flinging herself off and landing perfectly in her high heels.

Leah was in her element; she couldn't stop looking around and giggling. Hugh overheard Leah telling me that she wanted to try a lap dance. She was so drunk I thought she was joking but Hugh took her request very seriously. Neither of us had witnessed a lap dance before, and the idea piqued my interest more than I cared to admit—not for any sexual reason but rather I was simply intrigued by what it entailed. Hugh looked up and nodded to the owner, and moments later three strippers approached our table in flawless gowns of gold, white and blue clinging effortlessly to their incredible figures.

'Pick one,' Hugh called out to Leah, and she looked at him almost dumbfounded. I could tell that she was unsure whether he was serious but she decided to throw caution to the wind and picked the glamorous caramel blonde in the gold dress. I looked at Hugh, not sure what was going on—I was still extremely intoxicated—but he pulled me closer to him and whispered in my ear.

'You're not getting one, so don't even think about it,' he said with a straight face.

I was a little taken aback: he was denying me something I hadn't even asked for, and that drove me insane. No man was going to tell me what I could or couldn't have! 'And why not?' I said in a frosty tone.

He returned my gaze as a sneaky smile crept across his face. He was enjoying seeing me get mad. He leaned in ever so close to me, brushed my neck with the tip of his thumb and whispered in my ear. 'Because I want you to enjoy giving me one later.' His voice was laced with the sexual tension we both knew was hanging between us and my frosty demeanour melted immediately. I was turned on, the skin-on-skin contact driving me crazy as I felt the slippery wetness of my sex amplify at the roughness in his voice. My inhibitions had disappeared and I was desperate to have him right then and there. He saw the desire in my eyes and his expression matched it. I looked down to the hand he was still holding but I was distracted from my train of thought as he placed his finger and thumb on my chin, lifted it and kissed me on the lips gently before his thumb trailed down my neck, brushing my collarbone. I choked in the air between us, unclasped our hands and rubbed the traces of his touch that had set fire to my skin. As I pulled away he cupped my chin and mouthed,

'I want you, and I want the chance to explain.' In that instant every bad thought left my head and I forgave him.

I watched on as Leah sat stone-still while the stripper started to grind up against her. It made me laugh as Leah fumbled with her hands, not knowing what to do with them or if she was even allowed to touch the other woman. I felt as though this night was going to be full of so many firsts for me, but I couldn't shake the feeling that I was doing the wrong thing, even though I hadn't really done anything yet.

I was itching to head out on to the dance floor as the music pumped through my veins but Hugh stopped me from leaving, so I stood up and began to dance with Leah after her lap dance. Hugh came up behind me and placed his hands firmly on my hips. I turned around in my drunken haze to face him, the music fading as the steely look of hunger in his eyes made me oblivious to everyone and everything around us. I felt the burning hot rigid length of him through his pants, pressed flat against my stomach as we melded further into the crowd surrounding us in the upstairs VIP area.

The heat radiating from his body was palpable. I swallowed hard in sweet anticipation. Despite the fear of the unknown and the building anxiety over losing my virginity, I knew, I could just feel it in my bones, that the night was going to end with pure and utter sheet-clawing, toe-curling, mind-blowing sex . . . lust at its greatest height until well after dawn. His stamina was incredible and his insatiable appetite for connection was something I was learning to crave. The copious amounts of alcohol I had consumed had lowered my inhibitions to the point where I was up for almost anything to heighten our mutual pleasure. We were finally in a good place, and my fight-or-flight instinct had been well and truly numbed.

I was steeling myself against the fervid desire to rip off his shirt and run my nails down his bare back, as he squeezed my hips tighter to the beat of the music, eyeing me off, daring me to act on animal instinct. I caught myself absentmindedly biting my bottom lip, which in turn drove him close to the edge. The authority in his tone, the electric touch and the suggestive looks between us all night had built me up to believe that our night was going to end exactly as I wanted, with him in charge . . . and on top.

When we finally left I was a mess. I was blind drunk and Leah was nowhere to be found. I had no intention of leaving her, and when I went outside I found her talking to—and pretty much all over—a stranger. So much for my wing-woman who was going to protect me from making the stupid decision of sleeping with Hugh.

We packed her into the car and got her upstairs to the apartment, where she promptly passed out. Now the effect of the alcohol had started to wear off and Leah was out of the picture, I grew scared of what was to come. Hugh had no idea that I was still a virgin or had been abused as a child.

I couldn't bring myself to admit the effect that it had on me, let alone tell someone else about it. Petrified that I didn't feel completely in control of myself or my surroundings, I went out on the balcony and lit up a cigarette, closed my eyes and hoped Hugh would pass out—but even in my state I realised there was no chance of that happening.

I kept my gaze determinedly on the ocean as he came out to join me, sitting on the sofa opposite me as I lay on the long pool chair with my cigarette hanging over the railing. In one swift motion he was up and next to me, his hands grasping my face and his lips kissing me passionately. I didn't move, I could barely even return his kiss as my heart began to race. I desperately wanted to be with him, to feel him inside me, but I was too afraid of the consequences in my head the next day if that happened. Without removing his lips from mine, he climbed up next to me on the lounge chair, placing his hands on my hips and pulling me on top of him. I panicked and rolled on to my back before he rolled on top and hovered over my body. He looked me in the eyes and whispered, 'Don't move, just close your eyes and trust me.'

Every fibre of my being wanted to jump up and run away from him, but something in his tone made me feel a little safer.

I looked at him, forgetting the cigarette I was holding over the balcony. I closed my eyes and, reluctantly, decided to trust him. For what felt like hours I waited for the worst to come, for him to touch me and for the feeling of panic to overwhelm me, until I finally felt his fingers gently trace lines across my face.

I relaxed a little as I felt his lips on my neck distracting me as his free hand slipped underneath me and pulled me to his chest. I couldn't move, I couldn't breathe; all I knew was that I wouldn't allow my fears to rule me anymore . . . or would I?

We were both fully clothed; he was still in his business shirt and jeans while I was in my little black dress and feeling as limp as a rag doll, my adrenaline pumping alongside my endorphins. As his knee separated my legs I knew I wanted him as much as he wanted me. His lips locked with mine again as he tightened his grip around my stomach and I felt myself wanting more as his hand ran up and down my thigh, lifting my dress ever so slightly.

Sheer terror and pure excitement battled within me but I still didn't move. I returned his hungry kiss as his hands began to explore my body, my fear starting to make me shake uncontrollably. I knew at any moment that the feeling of panic was due to set in and that my first instinct would be to run away. In that moment I remembered the feeling of violation all over again as I battled to keep Hugh's face in my mind's eye, forgetting anyone who had ever forcefully touched me before and trying to focus on the fact that this was someone I was *allowing* to touch me.

My eyes remained tightly shut as I felt his hand running higher up my thigh. Inside I was screaming *no* but I couldn't manage to utter the word. I knew that I wanted him to take things further but I couldn't fight back the fear growing inside. He peeled aside my G-string and began to rub my cleft with his thumb. I could feel myself growing aroused immediately, the excitement only intensified by the idea of being outside on the balcony and the possibility of being caught by Leah. His pace quickened as his pleasure intensified—I felt it in his kiss, in the growing length of him pressed firmly against my leg—and I threw my head back as I felt myself letting go, my mind growing clouded at the impending orgasm building inside me. He was reading me well and before I could protest he rammed his fingers inside me, tipping me over the edge as his pace matched my racing heart. I groaned in his kiss as his free hand ran through my hair, pulling it backwards so I could look him in the eyes as I climaxed. I squeezed my eyes shut tightly again as I felt the sweat clinging to my body and the ripples of pleasure intensifying, sending shivers down my spine. I was spent.

I lay in his arms holding back the tears that were stemming from the fears inside my heart that had, for the first time ever, not been able to consume me. He kissed my face and forehead gently before he lifted me out of the chair, cradling me in his arms and carrying me into the bedroom.

As I lay down on the bed, my eyes still closed, I feared that what I had unleashed was not going to stop. I wasn't sure if I was really ready to take that next step with him,

I felt I had pushed myself as far as I could and was afraid of the consequences if I didn't stop it there. The night ended in ecstasy but I didn't end up sleeping with him.

Hugh kept his promise; he didn't push my boundaries and didn't try anything any further. We kissed late into the night as I lay on his bare chest wearing my silk pyjama bottoms and black singlet that I couldn't even remember changing into. Out on the balcony I had felt his excitement brush up against me as he lay on top of me caressing my neck with sweet kisses, but in the bedroom never once did he try to push me any further or even try to explore the possibility of me sleeping with him.

The next morning I woke up in the same position in which I had fallen asleep: on his chest with my hand tracing lines on his skin as his thumb rubbed my shoulder and he kissed my forehead.

We didn't need to say another word to each other; it had all been said in our actions the previous night. If this was going to happen, it was going to happen on my terms . . . and my terms were yet to be determined.

•

I reluctantly said goodbye to Hugh. No matter how confused I was inside, there was still a big part of me that really didn't want to leave him. MTV was playing an Usher marathon, and as I hugged Hugh, 'Caught Up' began. The lyrics heightened my anxiety, because the previous twelve hours related in a way that I wasn't ready to admit. I would never have expected something like this to happen to me, but it had and now I didn't want to let him go. I was caught up and at the time I had no idea how much my feelings would intensify over the next few months.

Hugh walked Leah and me to the elevator and kissed me goodbye. The same electricity from his lips pierced through mine and into the depths of my soul.

As soon as we began the drive home I received a call from Hugh, telling me he wanted to see me again soon, and asking if I could fly out to see him. I was a little apprehensive about spending more time with him until I got my head sorted, but at the same time I couldn't help but feel a little excited.

'I would love to see you again soon,' he said, sounding so calm while on the inside I was a mess.

'Let me see what I have planned and I'll let you know.' Even as I said the words I knew that I was going to make the time to fly out to see him. It was becoming almost impossible not to want to see him, especially after our night together.

As soon as we hung up I turned to Leah and said, 'Feel like repeating last night in another town?' She took one look at me and nodded as a huge cheeky grin crept across her face. We began to make plans on the drive, and within two weeks we were on our way there.

#SixthConfession

#COAMMPlaylist:

'Behind These Hazel Eyes'

Kelly Clarkson

During the two weeks away from Hugh my feelings for him solidified and the flirtatious butterflies went into overdrive. We communicated daily and I grew to see a beautiful side of this man as he opened up and gave me a little more insight into his life. Some people in the industry saw him as a dark but loveable underworld character because he stayed out of the media eye, while others thought he was trouble; the reality was he didn't let many people into his inner circle.

When Leah and I flew into town we decided to spend the first two days together just enjoying ourselves. It was the first time Leah had been to that town and it was the first time I had been there without my family. We decided we were going to paint the town red. We had rented an apartment in the city, and because we had caught a late flight and landed at 10.30 p.m., we went straight to the apartment and crashed.

Over the next two days we had the time of our lives: days at the markets and beach, nights in fantastic bars and restaurants drinking too much and making new best friends.

The first day we walked for an hour along the beach until the sky turned from bright and sunny to black and wet in the span of ten minutes. We decided to stop into a bar and have a few drinks—and I have to say, it's now one of my favourite bars in that town. It's nothing more than a hole in the wall but the memories we made there will last a lifetime.

We sat at a table outside as the rain poured around us and the traffic slowed to a halt because of the conditions. In front of us were two gentleman also enjoying a few drinks, and after Leah and I had grown a little tipsy we decided to interrupt their conversation. The two men ended up joining us, and for the next nine hours we all became the best of friends and continued to drink and enjoy the view. I can't say I remember much of what happened but I do know that we got quite drunk and ended up hitting on the gorgeous bartender and took a lot of photos to remember his beautiful physique. To top it all off I was proposed to by a Frenchman; I quickly accepted and we began to plan our honeymoon. Our fun afternoon moved into one of our best nights ever.

We ended up walking home, and after Leah got us lost we finally made it back to our apartment, where we had every intention of going out again—but instead we both passed out.

The next morning Leah had a massive hangover and didn't want to go anywhere, but I insisted we make the most of the day. We enjoyed a beautiful lunch and walked around the city before returning to our home-away-from-home to get ready for another night out. When we were finally ready— fabulous outfits, perfect hair and make-up—we headed to a magnificent bar with a massive staircase out the front in one of the worst and most dangerous neighbourhoods in the city. One section of the neighbourhood had been made famous by a movie a few years earlier and its bright red light can be seen from halfway across the city. When we first arrived, the bar was full, but my feet were killing me from walking all day and after thirty minutes we found a space. About three seconds later two moderately attractive guys squeezed in next to us and started to chat to us. They pulled out novelty male appendage straws and we immediately laughed as they began to drink from them. Other diners turned around and looked in disgust, but for the next two hours we had a great time with our new friends.

Not long after, we moved from the bar into the club section of the venue, where Leah ended up making out with one of the guys. The other guy turned to me, leaned in and whispered, 'So, if we're going to hook up we should probably get out of here now, but you can't stay the night because I have to be up early, so . . . yeah.'

I don't know if I was more disgusted or angry, but I immediately stood up and spoke to him coldly. 'There was never *any* chance of that happening!' I stormed off before he had the chance to respond.

I was appalled, and all I could think was that if this was what the dating scene entailed, count me out. I felt degraded and was royally pissed off—he hadn't even offered to buy me a drink! Not that it would have made a difference, but it showed me that he didn't even have a basic level of courtesy.

When I reached the bathroom I pulled out my phone and saw a missed call from Hugh. Immediately I felt a bit better, and I called him back, desperate to hear his beautifully soothing voice. The more the male species let me down the easier it was for me to fall back into Hugh's arms.

'Hey, stranger,' I said when he answered.

'Hey, babe, where are you?' Hugh responded. I could hear in his voice that something was off. He sounded a little sick.

'In the city. Come out and join me,' I almost begged.

'I wish I could, bub, but I'm not feeling well.'

'Oh, that sucks. I wish you could be here.'

'Are you and Leah having fun?' He still sounded a little off and this time I knew it wasn't because he was sick, it was something else.

'Yeah, it's been great. We met a couple of guys and Leah is totally into one of them, so I'm enjoying the night because she is. You should get some rest, though. I can't wait to see you tomorrow.' I tried to sound upbeat when I felt nothing of the sort. There was a pause on the other end of the line and I knew that he wasn't happy about the situation, but neither was I—I didn't want to be out with any other guy, I wanted to be out with him.

'Be safe, if you need anything call me,' he demanded, a little frostier than I think he intended. I was beginning to appreciate his protectiveness, but I didn't like feeling that my choices were being taken away from me, which only added to my nerves and confusion about where things were leading with him.

We hung up and I returned to find Leah locking lips with the guy she had been hanging off all night, so I tried to relax and returned to the bar, where I spotted my 'friend' chatting up another girl. I felt a tap on my shoulder and turned to find Leah and her new friend behind me. We ordered a drink and then in my infinite tipsy wisdom I decided it was time for payback. I walked over to where the disrespectful prick was standing ogling the girl and interrupted.

'Oh, here you are, honey. Did you want a cigarette?' As I produced it I stood next to him and he took it, smiling at me. The girl looked straight at me, and clearly she was unimpressed.

'Ugh, I think you've made your point,' she said before stalking off. He was gobsmacked and I had achieved my goal: cock-blocking mission initiated, and he deserved it.

A few minutes later I ran after the girl and apologised. I explained what had happened and told her that she would be making a mistake if she went anywhere near that creep.

'Thank you,' she said when I had finished. She smiled and hugged me before walking over to a group of girls, where— judging by their sniggers and looks in the guy's direction—she obviously told the entire story. The story soon spread around the club, and I can confidently say he didn't end up getting laid that night. All I can say is, don't mess with Ava Reilly!

A little later I made my way to the bathroom to fix my hair, but I didn't expect what happened next. My phone fell out of my clutch, and when I picked it up I saw five missed calls from Hugh and a text message that ended up saying it all.

I have tried to call you but instead you're probably hooking up with some other guy!

My happy mood was instantly trashed. This was the second time in one night that someone had pretty much called me a slut, and I was far from it. I could handle it coming from someone who didn't know me, but when it came from Hugh it broke my heart. In my infinite drunken wisdom I immediately tried to call him back to let him know how pissed off I was, but the call went to voicemail, so I left a message giving him a piece of my admittedly spinning mind. I then threw my phone into my bag and refused to look at it again.

I flung open the bathroom door and headed towards Leah to tell her what had happened. As soon as I told her I wanted to leave she agreed, and her new friend Toby drove us back to our apartment. Without even asking he came up with her, which annoyed me because I really wanted to be alone, but I felt rude telling him to leave. Before we had arrived we had made one rule—no guys in the room we were sharing—and I hoped Leah wouldn't break it.

As soon as I opened the door and walked into the bathroom I considered locking myself in there until after he left. I was so upset, and after I washed my face and walked out into the bedroom I was livid to find that she had taken him in there and they had started to make out on my bed!

I'd had enough. I wanted to catch the first flight out and never return. I began to pack my things and slam every door I could find. I knew that I was behaving irrationally but I couldn't help but feel that Leah had betrayed me too that night. I needed fresh air and wasn't going to be able to clear my head with the two of them going at it like rabbits. I grabbed my keys and walked downstairs for a cigarette, but not before I made a point of slamming the front door.

I reached the glass front doors and pushed them open, gasping in the cold night air. As soon as I sat down on the stone steps I pulled out my earphones and pressed play on my

phone. The next song shook me to the core; it was exactly
how I felt about Hugh and my biggest fear summed up in
the most beautiful melody and lyrics: Amy Winehouse's
acoustic rendition of 'Will You Still Love Me Tomorrow?'
I felt myself slipping deeper and deeper into the endless pit
as tears streamed down my face and my frail body shook.
I realised that I wasn't really angry that Leah had brought a
guy home. I was pissed off that I was jealous; I was so hurt
and angry with myself because all I kept thinking was why
couldn't I be normal like that? Why couldn't I just sleep with
someone? Why couldn't I be like anyone else my age and not
be afraid? I cried for everything that had been taken from
me at such a young age and because I didn't know how to
change it . . . I didn't know how to be normal.

After my cigarette and Amy Winehouse's soulful melody
I felt calmer. I stood up, brushed myself off and tried to put a
smile back on my face, but it didn't last; I couldn't stop the tears
and the anger from returning. I turned and walked through
the glass doors, ready to march upstairs and give Leah and
Toby a piece of my mind, but as the elevator doors opened,
there they were. Leah took one look at my tear-stained face
and told him to leave.

I looked at her and felt my hard exterior crumble along
with everything else inside me as she pulled me towards her
and squeezed me in a hard embrace. We moved back into the
elevator and I dropped to the floor and cried again. I couldn't

figure out how my night had turned from fun to horrible, but it felt like one of the lowest points in my life.

Leah got me back into the apartment. I walked straight into the lounge room and lit up a cigarette. After more uncontrollable crying she finally convinced me to open up. I told her everything, about my past, about Hugh—everything she needed to know to understand what I was going through. We talked for most of the night. She apologised and I apologised, and eventually I fell asleep crying silent tears into my pillow as the darkness finally consumed me.

I woke up the next morning with a killer headache. I didn't want to get out of bed but I knew I had to pull myself together and make the most of the new day ahead of me. When Hugh called he apologised over and over, but I wouldn't hear any of it. The only thing we could agree on was that we needed to see each other to talk, so we decided to meet for dinner. In the meantime, Leah and I left the apartment early and decided to take a walk—a walk that lasted nine kilometres. It was good to get out into the fresh air, enjoying the incredible parklands and being able to reflect on everything that had happened, but by the end of it my feet were killing me because I did it in heels!

I was nervous about Leah seeing Hugh again after our conversation the night before. I didn't want her to feel like the third wheel, so I told her to invite Toby from the night before. I knew I needed an excuse to be alone with Hugh and keeping Leah occupied was the best way to achieve this.

A few hours later as we all arrived at Hugh's office building, I was starting to regret my decision to see him. I knew we weren't going to be able to sort out our situation in just one evening and I had a massive hangover, which didn't help my state of mind.

As we walked into his offices I was in awe; every inch of the place screamed success. Evidence of his career achievements were placed strategically on the walls. The moment we saw each other I knew I couldn't be angry with him, but I couldn't just let it go either. He placed his hand on my back and kissed my cheek before turning to greet Leah and Toby. I kept watching him as he showed us around and proudly took us into his office, which, I was shocked to see, was pretty much an apartment, complete with kitchen, bathroom (which included a shower) and lounge room.

Leah and her new beau took a seat in the lounge room while Hugh walked into his office. There was something in the air that drew me towards him and I followed him blindly. As I entered the room I knew he had sensed me following and turned straight around, stopping dead in his tracks to stare at me. I stood, frozen, for about thirty seconds before my eyes began to well with tears. He took a step closer and I took a step back before hurriedly wiping the tears from my eyes. Not a word was exchanged as we stood facing each other blankly. In one swift movement he was in front of me with his arms clasped gently around me, and the tears poured out of me, with violent trembles erupting from my shoulders. My legs went to mush and if he hadn't been holding me I would have sunk to the floor.

'I am *so* sorry,' he whispered in my ear as he tightened his grip around me. 'I just couldn't bear the thought of you with anyone else and I got jealous. I really didn't want to hurt you.'

My tears started to ease along with my erratic breathing. 'I can't keep doing this,' I managed to say. 'I need to know what I'm doing with you or we stop this, now.' It was all I could muster as I took a step back from him, wiping my eyes and trying to compose myself.

He ran his hand through his hair and sighed. The words he had once said to me echoed around us: he didn't date younger women because they always became clingy and it wasn't worth the headache. I knew it was time I started being honest with myself and with him, so I prepared myself for whatever it was he was going to say.

'I don't know what this is yet,' he said. 'I can't figure it or you out and it's driving me up the wall. I don't want you to be with anyone else but I just don't know what I feel. I know it's not fair, but I want you all to myself. I need to see you more, I need to be around you and I need to figure this out with you,' he said as he walked towards me again.

I took another step back as he came closer, and his face showed his concern—clearly he knew I was ready to run.

I looked straight through him while I tried to gather my thoughts.

'Why do women have to complicate things?' He responded in my absence of words.

My eyes darted towards him. 'You have no right to speak to me like that, I'm not one of the hordes of women throwing themselves at you. If you want me to wait for you to figure yourself out, then you better give me a bloody good reason!' I spat.

He looked at me with sorrow in his eyes and said, 'Ava, there is a lot to consider here and I am more concerned for you than for myself. I haven't ever been this consumed by someone before and I don't want to label it. The last time I put a name to what I was feeling it didn't turn out so well. I don't want to hurt you, and I don't want to lose you.'

'Hugh, you can't have your cake and eat it too!'

'Ava, I really like you, I want to spend time with you and I want to do it exclusively—isn't that enough for now?' he said, pleading for it to be enough.

I put my head in my hands and took a deep breath in before I heard him speak again. 'I'm falling for you, Ava, and I'm scared I'm going to hurt you.'

I opened my eyes and walked towards him, unsure even then of how I was going to respond. I was conflicted with so many different feelings but somehow I managed to push anything negative out of my mind and for once in my life try to focus on something positive in a very messy situation. I felt the truth as it poured from his soul; he was in turmoil.

'Hugh, I can live with that for now, but I'm not going to be at your beck and call. I have a life and you can't try to control me or I will walk away.'

He placed his arms around me and exhaled before whispering, 'I promise I won't.'

A few minutes later we returned to join Leah and Toby before heading to dinner. I tried to put some distance between Hugh and me, but I found it almost impossible with the magnetic pull beckoning me to his side as we walked towards the restaurant. Since our first meeting I hadn't really thought through the repercussions of being seen with him in public—I had always made sure I had someone else with me so that it didn't draw the wrong kind of attention, but this time my head was going into overdrive. I was nervous at the thought of being seen together let alone photographed, so knowing that we had other people with us made it a little easier to explain away in my head.

When we finally reached the restaurant Hugh could sense that I was feeling uncomfortable and during the entire meal he held my hand under the table; he refused to let go no matter what protests I tried to throw at him.

After we ate, a small argument erupted between Hugh and Toby over who was going to pay. I knew not to argue with Hugh about money and I didn't have the energy to fight, so I kept quiet as they argued it out. Of course, Hugh won.

After dinner another argument began over who would take us to the airport for our flight home. I knew I would see Hugh soon, so I stepped in and said goodbye to him. On the drive to the airport with Toby that evening I kept silent and put my shades on while tears ran down my cheeks. As we drove away from Hugh's building I could feel the distance growing quickly in my heart. Leah turned to look at me and knew what I was feeling without me having to speak.

'He loves you, Ava,' said Toby as we neared the departures drop-off. 'It was so obvious in the way he looked at you the entire night, the way he spoke to you. I haven't seen someone look at another person that way before. It was like he couldn't stop himself, he *had* to look at you and be near you.'

I struggled to fight back the tears that were building up again; I was no clearer on what I was going to do and it was eating me up inside.

'Don't,' Leah said, looking pointedly at him.

'But you love him as well, I can see it's killing you,' was the last thing he said to me before I climbed out of the car.

When we boarded the plane I plugged my earphones into the television and tuned out the other passengers. I felt bare.

Neither Leah nor I would be the same after that trip, and we both returned home with tears pouring from the inside out, from the very depths of our souls, but for very different reasons.

#SeventhConfession

#COAMMPlaylist:

'U Got it Bad'

Usher

The next few months after I returned home from my trip interstate I had a hard time coming to terms with everything. So much had happened between Hugh and me in such a short period of time and I was no clearer on where I stood with him, but I knew I couldn't let him go. I was feeling a little lost, and I couldn't quite put a finger on what was going on inside me. Since we had met we had spent so much time together on both a professional and personal level that it was becoming even more difficult to keep track of my emotions. One night Hugh called me to ask me what I was doing for Christmas and New Year's Eve. I told him that I would be spending it with family, and he sounded really down as we talked. I had only known him for ten months and I think he sensed that I wasn't ready to introduce him to my family, so he asked if I would take a few days out to see him over Christmas if he flew into town. I wasn't sure I wanted to see him, let alone spend time with him over such an important holiday, but I also knew that I really needed to see where this was going, so I agreed.

As Christmas approached I became more and more nervous and emotional. I knew that it wouldn't be long until things would become intimate between us, but I wasn't sure if I was ready. A week before Christmas I began to get excited—until that fateful day when Hugh called and told me he wouldn't be able to make it because he had to go overseas with his children. I was both disappointed and relieved.

I knew I needed some distance between us, and as Christmas and New Year's Eve passed I began to find myself in a place of comfort over the situation with Hugh. I realised that I needed to give myself a break; I wasn't the one who had made marriage vows and even though I knew I was playing with fire, I came to accept that I couldn't help whom I had begun to fall for. This rollercoaster of emotions was wearing me down to the point where I knew I was going to end up at a fork in the road: one path would lead to self-destruction, and the other to the point of no return by Hugh's side. Either way, I had to make my choice and stick with it, consequences and all.

As January rolled on I became busier as each day passed and I found it hard to find the time to stop and enjoy life, let alone spend time with Hugh. It wasn't until February that we finally had a chance to catch up, and this time everything was different. We had grown individually in the short time apart and being together seemed to be the choice we had both made.

Exactly a year after we met, on 12 February, we agreed to meet up at his beachside apartment again. As the day finally arrived my stomach began to tie itself in knots, and I was tempted to back out. It wasn't the fact that I was going to be around him that had me on edge, it was the fact that I was going to be around him alone, and we both knew what that would mean. I still hadn't told Hugh about my past or that I was a virgin, and I really wasn't in a hurry to, either, but I could feel myself trying to come to terms with what was destined to happen between us, not only on a physical level but also an emotional level.

I arrived at his apartment at 7.30 that night but I couldn't bring myself to announce my arrival straightaway; instead of calling him I decided to take a walk along the beach to clear my head and get a grip. My hands were shaking as I realised how close he was; I knew what was going to happen that night and I had prepared myself physically for it, but mentally I was scrambling to comprehend how the hell I was going to handle it. Hugh had never tried to push me into anything that I didn't want to do, he was kind, attentive and gentle with me in every single aspect, and I knew I would end up sleeping with him that night. As I sat on the sand and watched the water caress the shoreline in the black night sky I tried to understand why this was such a big deal to me. He had done everything right, everything to earn my trust, and yet it still didn't seem like enough to make me feel confident giving him the last part of innocence I had left in my control. I closed my eyes and took deep breaths in to try to soothe the angst growing inside me, which started to help—until I felt my phone vibrate against my leg and I almost jumped out of my skin. I pulled it out and fumbled with it, dropping it in the sand. When I was finally able to pick it up I saw Hugh's name on the caller ID.

'Hello?' I answered, trying desperately to rein in my fear.

'Hey, babe. Where are you?' he responded with a smile in his voice that melted away a little of my anxiety.

'I'm almost there, just taking a walk along the beach,' I said, hoping that he wouldn't ask why; I didn't have an answer for myself let alone for him.

'Well, get your arse up here quickly. I want to see you!' I could hear that he was excited, and I hoped he wouldn't expect me to jump into bed with him straightaway, because I needed to work myself up to it.

'Okay, I won't be too much longer.' I knew I had no more time to sit here stuffing around—he knew where I was and if I didn't hurry up he would come down to the beach to find me.

'Okay. See you soon.' The soothing confidence in his voice

melted me to the core. It was then that I realised I was doing the right thing.

I lit a cigarette as I hung up, turned around and looked up at the building behind me. I could see his apartment on the top floor and knew at that moment he was up there waiting for me. The light was on and I could see the very spot we had first become intimate; it sent shivers down my spine as I closed my eyes and relived the delicious memory—it was so vivid, just the thought of his lips on my neck was enough to send me over the edge again. As I opened my eyes slowly I found myself looking at the same spot, thinking . . . am I ready for this?

I opened the glass doors and walked in with my Louis Vuitton handbag hanging on my arm and my overnight suitcase following closely behind me. I could feel sweat creep into my palms and my body tremble as I stepped into the waiting elevator. In mere seconds the doors flew open and I walked across the short hallway before knocking gently on Hugh's door.

Immediately the door flung open and an immaculately dressed Hugh threw his arm around my waist and pulled me close to him, kissing me passionately. As his hand ran up and down my back, I felt my heart race and the knot in my stomach quickly melted into a burning desire for him. He smelled incredible and the firm grip he had on me took my breath away. I pulled away, gasping for air moments later and he allowed me to pass before shutting the door quietly behind him. I didn't wait for an invitation, I walked into the master bedroom to put my things away. I could feel him behind me as I placed my bags on the bed, and before I had the chance to let go of the handle he came up behind me and twirled me around to kiss me again. I put my arms around his neck and ran my fingers through his hair, the spark returning instantly along with feelings of uncertainty but I fought the urge to pull away.

I giggled when he finally let me go—I didn't know what I was laughing at but it calmed me a little.

'I'll give you a few minutes if you want to have a shower and get ready, but be quick, we have dinner reservations,' he said firmly. The command in his voice was laced with kindness, but I felt my free will bending to please him.

As he left I pulled out a pair of jeans, a black crystal-encrusted halter top and a cream jacket, along with a pair of killer heels. I didn't know where we were going but I wanted to look my best.

Twenty minutes later I was made up and ready to go. The moment I turned to take in the full picture of my outfit in the mirror, I found my self-confidence. I took hints from style icons like Kim Kardashian and knew how to accentuate the curves of my voluptuous figure by choosing the most flattering styles to suit my body, and in doing so I knew I was going to feel comfortable no matter what or whom I faced—this time I was prepared to stake my claim against anyone who wanted to challenge it.

I walked out of the room with my head held high, and as I turned the corner Hugh sensed my presence and turned around from behind the sofa to greet me. I stopped abruptly as his jaw fell open.

'Is it too much?' I asked, feeling my earlier confidence waver.

'You look . . . beautiful,' he stammered.

'Thank you. Are you ready to go?' I responded, desperately wanting to leave the apartment. I was pleasantly surprised by his compliment—I hadn't been expecting it and was used to shying away from male praise—but somehow it made me feel a little calmer. Not calm enough, however, to want to stay in the apartment alone with him any longer. I knew that I needed a clear head to prepare for my night ahead with Hugh and being alone with him right then was making it too hard to focus.

'I'm not sure I want to go out now,' he teased, his tone undercut with pure desire.

'Well, we can't back out now,' I said, knowing I was driving him crazy . . . and loving every minute of it.

As we walked to dinner I felt a warmth building inside me. The restaurant was very classy and was named after one of the most prestigious districts in the heart of New York City. The clean black-and-white lines drew me in, and I knew right then and there that this was going to be an incredibly special night. We were out in public, and my subconscious kept reminding me that Hugh wasn't hiding me away, which made me hope that he *was* separated from his wife as he had told me—surely if they were still together he would be careful and wouldn't walk down the street or into the restaurant holding my hand. The only possible dampener for the night would be if we ran into any of his earlier conquests. I had no idea how extensive the list was but it was becoming a touchy point for me.

I had fought with myself for so long, trying to clear my conscience and get to the bottom of my feelings for Hugh, but with everything I was feeling and the fact that I was finally moving into a point where I was semi-comfortable with a man for the first time in a long time, I was afraid of what his response would be, and what the consequences would be for me.

Before I even had the chance to ask Hugh where he would like to sit the manager came over to us. My gaze dropped to the ground; I hoped we could have a little privacy, because I really needed to keep my head in the game to prepare myself for the night ahead, and being around other people seemed to make me lose focus. I had to remind myself that this was what I had to expect if I decided to enter into something intimate with a man who was extremely well known and respected; the invasion of privacy came as part of the package. It also made me realise that no matter how big my clients were, I never wanted to be recognisable; I could never be famous. I valued my anonymity too much.

I had made a judgement call before I arrived that I wasn't going to drink too much. I had a meeting with a client the next morning, and I wanted to stay in control—what I was discovering, though, was that this was almost impossible when I was around Hugh. Being with him in such a public forum made my confidence falter. As we sat down the manager took our order and we were finally left alone. I looked out at the vast space around us and it finally hit me how public our presence was. There were patrons everywhere looking in our direction; I instantly felt self-conscious and yet I didn't feel I could voice any of my concerns to Hugh. Even though the age difference between us meant nothing to me, I was afraid that it did mean something to him, based on what he had said months earlier about why he didn't date younger women. I didn't want him to see me as immature, or as another Pain that he had to deal with, so I decided it was best to keep my thoughts to myself.

Soon our meals were served, and I sat silently as the restaurant manager joined us and began conversing with Hugh. I had met him once before and he seemed as lovely as usual, but I was uncomfortable. It didn't look like Hugh even realised. As our plates were taken away by the attentive staff, the first round of drinks arrived. I stuck with a vodka and orange, because I knew it was the one drink that wouldn't get me totally smashed if I drank a few of them.

I didn't want to be anti-social but I really needed to be alone for a few minutes. I ventured to the bathrooms and found myself staring at the reflection in the mirror; I barely recognised her. The woman in the mirror looked amazing and confident, but I felt insecure, upset and completely irrational. I knew what it was that was eating at me: I was petrified at the thought of finally having sex with Hugh at the end of the night. I felt as if I owed it to him after all the time he had invested in me, but I still wasn't really ready. I was holding tightly on to the only scrap of innocence I had left—it wasn't as though I didn't want to trust Hugh with my virginity, I couldn't bring myself to believe that he wouldn't end up hurting me in the long run.

When I returned, two shots of Gran Patrón Burdeos tequila sat on the table and the manager was nowhere to be seen. Hugh smiled and pushed the shot towards me gently. I eyed off the glass with caution. I had never had tequila before—was I really about to start now when I had promised myself I wouldn't drink much?

I swallowed hard and leaned over to pick up the salt. I took a deep breath in and licked the skin in between my thumb and index finger before shaking a small amount of salt onto it, and then I picked up the lime wedge in the same hand and the shot in my free hand.

I braced myself for whatever was to come, then licked the salt off, lifted the liquid to my lips and downed the contents of the glass at the same time as Hugh. I felt the fire erupt down my throat and circle in my stomach as I sucked on the lime wedge. I could feel the cloud of self-preservation and judgement wash away as a clean level of calmness enveloped me. I looked straight at Hugh and realised that was why he had ordered the shots: he knew I needed to take the edge off but he wasn't going to openly embarrass me by mentioning it. Instead, he placed his hand gently on mine and smiled. I instantly felt at ease. The shot had done the trick; I wasn't scared anymore, I was calmer and, I like to think, a lot more fun. As the night rolled on more and more people approached our table, and I didn't mind because by this point I had thrown my original plan out the window and was well on my way to becoming inebriated. I actually welcomed the company.

As Hugh answered a call on his mobile, a man sat next to me and introduced himself as the restaurant owner. We began to talk and got along quite well. When I finished my vodka and orange he asked if I was interested in trying a new wine they had just imported. In my drunken state I stood up, squeezed Hugh's hand and mouthed that I was heading to the bar, the owner following after me. As I stood at the bar trying the new drink, I could see Hugh from behind a huge white pillar. He was still on his call and I was enjoying the view I had from the bar; he looked delicious in his unbuttoned business shirt and dark blue jeans. I could feel the growing desire burning from the inside out as I sipped the wine.

The more I drank the harder it was for me to stand still. I was getting antsy and felt like dancing. I desperately wanted to feel Hugh grind up against me in a crowd of sweaty people—better yet I wanted to get hot and sweaty with him between the sheets.

When Hugh finally joined us I was standing against the Italian pillar and the owner was leaning against the bar talking to me. I was midway through a conversation and by this stage seriously drunk when Hugh grabbed my hand and said we had to go.

I laughed out loud at how serious he was, but something in his cool tone and tight grip made me shut up pretty quickly. He dragged me out of the restaurant on to the kerb that was filled with waiting patrons, where he stopped dead in his tracks and spun around.

'I don't like that!' he said almost inaudibly with a roughness in his voice that I hadn't heard before.

'What?' I responded with a smile, trying to keep the situation light because I could feel the intensity of his frustration burning in my direction.

'I don't like seeing you with other men—the way he was looking at you, the way he was coming on to you, the way you were laughing at what he was saying. I just don't like it.

Why aren't you that easy around me? You're always so tense,' he spat, making my happy mood quickly dissipate.

'We were talking about *you*, for fuck's sake! The reason I was so comfortable around him was because I wasn't attracted to him!' I threw back at him. I was extremely pissed off by this point. He was ruining my night and I was very intoxicated, the combination throwing my emotions out of whack.

He froze, obviously not expecting my response to come out so confidently. The restaurant owner *was* stunning but he didn't have what Hugh had—it was then that I realised Hugh had my heart.

'Stop reading something into nothing. I'm here with you, aren't I?' I said after a few seconds, allowing the situation to settle with him.

I saw the conflict growing in his eyes. I reached up and planted a passionate kiss on his lips to reassure him.

'I'm so sorry, Ava,' he finally said.

Once the dust had settled we made our way down the street and ended up at the gentlemen's club we had been to before. I was excited to be there again—it held fond memories for me and I knew that Hugh would be able to calm down again once we were inside.

After bypassing security I met all of the owners but found myself getting along with the one I had met before. Rick was just as lovely this time and it was obvious that he adored Hugh.

Even though I was stupidly drunk I found myself having the time of my life and didn't want it to stop. I downed another shot and Hugh made sure the drinks kept coming. I felt myself slipping well and truly beyond drunk and into a state of severe intoxication but I really didn't care; I was having too much fun to remember that I had a meeting in less than eight hours.

As we all stood at the bar talking I realised just how low my inhibitions were when I announced to Rick that I didn't have a gag reflex. Both Hugh and Rick dropped their drinks right next to the bar and the glasses shattered on the floor as they burst out laughing. Rick looked at Hugh with huge eyes before saying, 'Is she for real?' Hugh couldn't stop laughing, and what happened next was something that I didn't realise I had done until it was far too late.

While both men stood there with their jaws dropped I turned to Rick and began the downward spiral of a conversation that I would later regret. I had never lowered myself this much in all my drunken experiences.

'Don't believe me, Rick? Why don't you find out for yourself?' I said confidently as I threw my head back and opened my mouth as wide as I could. The look on his face was priceless, he turned to Hugh who couldn't believe what he was seeing and burst into another fit of laughter. It felt so good to make him laugh, even if it was at my own expense.

Rick turned to look at me, not believing that I was serious until I raised my eyebrows at him, tempting him to give it a go. He reached out and stuck three fingers down my throat before wiggling them around for good measure.

'Holy shit, she's a keeper,' was all he could say when he finally removed his fingers from the back of my throat. I blushed, realising what I had just done and instantly felt guilty as I looked at Hugh. He shook his head and smiled at me as he downed the rest of his drink.

'Well, now I think I owe you a drink,' Rick said after composing himself.

'I think you do, I'm a little parched now,' I responded, trying to forget what I had just done.

I was having a great time until what seemed like the thirty-third drink, when I began to feel sick. I thought I had handled my alcohol pretty well despite my little throat trick; I could barely feel a thing and my mind was muted, which was both a good thing and a bad thing. Just as another round was ordered I felt that I had hit my limit. I leaned over the bar and asked the waitress for a glass of water instead of a vodka and orange. She could see the state I was in and politely handed me a glass of cold water, which I immediately downed. It was a big mistake and I knew that I was going to pay for it. I excused myself from the group and feigned a smile before I walked straight into the gold bathroom. I rushed into the closest stall, placed my bag on the back of the door, kneeled down and was very sick. Shortly after that I got up, laughed and then managed to redo my make-up. In my drunken state my fixed face looked perfect, but I took a photo to check what kind of a job I had done the next morning—just in case. I then popped a breath mint and rejoined Hugh.

When I finally returned the group was in full swing, laughing, smiling and carrying on. I knew I had hit a wall, so I took no notice of anyone and grabbed another glass of water. The only reason Hugh knew something was wrong was because instead of standing with them and joining in on the fun I chose to sit down opposite them.

Breaking away from the group, he walked straight over to me and said, 'I'll take you home, honey, you look like you could use some sleep.' I tried to argue with him because I didn't want to ruin his night but he wouldn't have a bar of it.

I barely remember leaving the club let alone getting back to the apartment. When we reached the front door he carried me into the bedroom, laid me gently on the bed and took off my shoes before turning on the television. I flipped over the covers and climbed under them into the cold bed.

'Ava, you can't sleep in that,' he said in a velvety smooth voice.

'Watch me,' I mumbled before cracking up laughing as I lay there obliterated. He kissed me gently on the forehead, and I didn't even register that he had left the room until after he returned with a glass of water and placed it on the bedside table next to me.

'I'll be back shortly. Rest up, I'm just going to give the keys to Rick. He's coming back for a drink in a few hours,' he whispered, which didn't surprise me, as he had mentioned Rick coming back to the apartment earlier in the evening. I had grown to realise that Hugh was a very social person and if he hadn't seen someone for a while, it seemed like he felt as though he owed them any time he could spare. I guessed it stemmed from the fact that most of his time was taken up by his office desk and iPhone, which was the price you pay for being successful, and something that I was learning quickly. I knew I would be okay in an hour, I was just exhausted—oh, and very, very drunk. After he left I tried to stay awake as long as I could. I felt so relieved because, despite my strong desires throughout the night, I was still conflicted and panic-stricken about actually going through with it and acting on them. My concerns began to ease a little as I thought I had escaped the possibility of intimacy . . . I had no idea how wrong I was as I finally fell asleep.

What felt like hours later I was woken up to a very bright light and someone standing by the bed. I didn't want to open my eyes. I wanted to slip back into blissful sleep, until I realised that I was hungry for Hugh's touch against my skin. I opened my eyes slowly, trying not to blind myself at the intruding light, and it wasn't until I looked up and saw a blonde Barbie standing over me, playing with my hair, that I began to panic. I recognised her immediately as Rick's girlfriend. Before my mind could register the fear my body felt she said in her cutesy little voice, 'You look so pretty when you sleep!'

My throat was so sore and dry that I couldn't scream. I thought I was in the middle of a nightmare, and I silently began to pray that I would wake up in a sweat and Hugh would be there to comfort me. When that didn't happen I sat up, jumped back and threw myself halfway across the bed. As my mind caught up I realised that I had taken off my clothes and found myself in my matching lace bra and underwear, so I grabbed the sheets and pulled my knees up to my chin as she edged closer.

At that moment the door flung open and Hugh entered to find me curled up on the corner of the bed as Barbie leaned over me giggling. The look of utter shock on his face gave me little comfort as I whimpered, 'What the fuck? Get her out of here.'

Within seconds he ordered her to leave and she began to laugh loudly, obviously drunk. I was paralysed in the corner of the bed, barely able to believe what had just happened. Hugh slid across the bed, kneeled next to me and gathered me up in his arms, hugging me in a fierce embrace. I felt my body convulse uncontrollably as the alcohol began to course through my veins again and the adrenaline made my heart race. Hugh may not have understood where my fears stemmed from but he had obviously sensed that there was something wrong. It was at that moment that I forced myself to look at him. I traced his jawline with my index finger and fought back the tears threatening to flow. I spun around to climb on top of him and began to kiss him passionately. I made the decision then that there was no way my mind was going to talk me out of it this time.

As my nerves and fears began to consume me I nevertheless felt like I was making the right decision. I kissed him passionately as I felt his hands run up and down my hips, the groan in his throat growing deeper and hungrier as I began to grind against him in soft but fluid motions. I felt the rigid length of him grow between my legs as my feeling of desire rushed to the depths of my sex, causing my muscles to spasm. He unclasped my bra and released my breasts, flinging the bra across the floor. The feeling of vulnerability flooded through me as he grasped my hips and flipped me underneath him before kissing my neck and down my collarbone. The burning electricity between us was becoming too much and I exhaled deeply as his mouth ventured south, leaving trails of light kisses along my stomach before stopping at my hips. He hooked his fingers under the fabric clinging to my skin and ripped it off. As the material tore I felt a rush of excitement run through me as the slick wetness returned with a vengeance. I arched my back in delightful anticipation before he slipped off the bed and walked into the bathroom. It was at that moment that panic set in and I curled up beneath the covers and flipped on to my stomach, trying to hide my face in the pillow.

Within moments he returned and climbed back on to the bed. He ran his hands down my back and then squeezed a cold liquid into his hands and began to massage in between my shoulder blades. The pain that erupted from his touch left me breathless. As I lay there silently feeling the tension release, the alcohol began to take effect again. I arched my back and turned around to face him. Much to my delight he was completely naked. I reached up and pulled him down towards me, running my nails along his back as I felt his arm wrap underneath me and pull me closer to him. I began nipping his ear before whispering that I was ready. With his free hand he tipped my head back to meet his gaze and his lips met mine again. I squeezed him tighter in frustrated but sweet anticipation. He pulled back before slowly gliding into me, filling me with his length. Ripples of ecstasy flowed through my body in a way that I had never known. He was a tight fit but the sound of his breath in my ear was enough to distract me. I felt his warm hands running down my neck towards my breasts and the intense gaze in his eyes sent violent trembles through my body as his pace quickened.

He placed his arm under my arched back and lifted me, kissing my neck ever so gently. I felt the fire inside my heart quicken into a roaring flame, burning me from the inside out. I felt empowered; I was in control and nothing was going to take away my newfound freedom from me. He set the edge of his jaw on my collarbone before whispering in my ear almost breathlessly.

'I promise not to break you.'

Those simple words consumed me as I let my inhibitions completely wash away and got caught up in the moment. While I was silent I kept my eyes closed to feel every gentle thrust, hear every breath and savour every moment. I exhaled, growing calmer as each minute passed. I felt the trust and bond between us grow and knew that this was more than a one-night stand.

Just as I began to feel the rush of desire pulsate through me, Rick knocked on the door and I snapped back to reality, freezing immediately as my pulse began racing with fear. In my drunken, euphoric state I had completely forgotten that he was even on the same continent let alone in the same apartment. In that moment I felt the fear break through my barrier of stability and I knew that there was no coming back. I grabbed the sheets and pulled them close as Hugh got up and walked towards the door. A flood of light entered the room, touching the darkest of corners but I couldn't concentrate. I couldn't stop the feeling of violation passing through me as I heard Hugh and Rick murmuring to the left of me. I was beginning to panic and couldn't focus on anything but the darkness ahead of me. I needed silence, I needed time to focus. I don't know how long I stayed in the spot but the numbness that had consumed my body was verging on the point of painful. I slid down beneath the covers and forced myself to close my eyes.

Once Rick left, Hugh returned to the blackened room but I pretended to be asleep. I couldn't move, I couldn't breathe, I was petrified of what was to come. He climbed across the bed and gathered me into his arms, rocking me back and forth kissing my forehead. I knew that he understood my unspoken fears; he may not have known where they stemmed from but he knew that there was something awfully wrong.

#EighthConfession

#COAMMPlaylist:

'All My Life'

K-Ci & JoJo

Lying in bed the next morning I rolled over to see that Hugh was still asleep. He looked so peaceful and I didn't want to wake him. He had his arms wrapped protectively around me, and while I was feeling a little suffocated I also felt safe.

As I listened to him breathe and watched his chest rise and fall the memories of our first night together flooded back through my mind. It was one of heated passion, and unlike anything I had experienced. I didn't really know what my expectations were when it came to relationships; was I more afraid of being loved or loving someone with everything I had? My fears stemmed from the physical and emotional pain of my past, but I was beginning to understand that my memories were something over which I had no control.

He had been sweet, kind, tender and gentle with my body, heart and soul. Our first night together was the most exciting, passionate and probably the healthiest thing I have ever done for myself. As we had begun to make love fear had controlled my body; I was trembling from the inside but on the outside time had stood still.

I had fallen asleep with Hugh's arms wrapped tightly around me but sometime in the middle of the night I had moved into my own space on the other side of the bed. I needed to be alone but didn't want to leave the safety I felt in his presence. It wasn't until I felt my arm being dragged towards him that I realised I had been crying in my sleep. I immediately resisted the pull and pushed all of my weight into the bed to stop from moving closer.

'Baby,' he had whispered, 'come here. I don't like the space between us. I want you in my arms.'

I had let him drag me closer, hoping I could find solace within his arms as they wrapped tightly around me again. Skin-to-skin contact was exactly what I needed, and I immediately felt safe and at home. I closed my eyes and concentrated on his breath blowing warmly on my neck before I finally drifted off into a peaceful and uninterrupted sleep.

As the sun rose I found myself in the same position but instead of being yanked out of a tear-stained sleep I was woken by soft kisses on my shoulder. The fear I knew I was supposed to register didn't exist; I wasn't afraid of his touch or his intentions as I let him consume me again. I felt the same safety and love as I had the night before, only this time I was very awake and alert.

'Morning, babe,' he whispered in my ear.

I didn't know what time it was but as soon as I moved I regretted it. I felt the impending hangover smash my body as the blinding light flowing in from the curtains reflected from the mirrored walk-in wardrobe at the end of the bed. I buried my head further into the crook of his arm until I spotted the glass of water beside the bed. I was desperate for the liquid to wet my painfully dry throat but I was too afraid to reach over and grab it. Even though I had drunk myself into oblivion the night before I maintained every memory and it made me smile to remember how many boundaries I had broken through.

'Good morning,' I said with a smile in my voice, barely recognising the horsey sound escaping from my mouth.

'Are you hungry?' he asked as I finally plucked up the courage to grab the glass on the bedside table. I hadn't felt hungry until that point but the thought of eating anything made me feel even more unwell.

'No, not really. Are you?' I responded as I swallowed the first gulp of water a little too quickly, resulting in hiccups.

'No, I actually just want to wrap you in my arms,' he said with a cheeky look in his eyes. I knew what that look was, I had seen it the night before. The first thought that crossed my mind was something I had never asked myself before: was I a morning sex kind of person?

As I set the glass of water back down on the bedside table he moved towards me and pulled me back down on to the bed. He leaned over my naked body as my head hit the pillow. I giggled as he began to smother me with kisses. I felt so carefree and happy—he may have taken my virginity but he had also given me back something I had never realised I was missing. He showered me with affection with no ulterior motive, and he gave me the chance to say no by sticking by his promise of never pushing my boundaries. I knew I was safe with him, and because of this I was ready to give him anything and everything.

When I stopped giggling he lifted his head to meet my gaze. With his faces inches from mine I was finally able to see a vulnerable side to him that until this point he had kept hidden. His eyes were so full of secrets but something about the way he looked at me—a vulnerability showing beneath the confident, hard exterior he portrayed to the world—made me feel like I was seeing him like no one else had.

His dark eyes were almost black, his features were striking and the strength of his fully flexed arms on either side of me gave me comfort, showing me he was strong enough to handle me at my worst, something he had seen part of the night before.

I lay silently for what felt like forever as I searched his eyes, and as he returned my stare I felt him piercing my own cold exterior, allowing me to share the raw person I was at heart. I reached my perfectly manicured thumb up to touch his cheek to wipe away an eyelash that had strayed. I felt him flinch beneath my fingertip and saw a flicker of the wall rising back up to protect him. After everything I had overcome the night before I couldn't let him withdraw from me. He turned his head but before he could unlock his eyes from me, my hands flew up to his face to straighten it back to where it had been moments before. Looking deeply into his eyes again I noticed something had changed. The playfulness had left his eyes, and his demeanour was less warm, but I wasn't going to break away just yet. I closed my eyes and pulled myself up to lock my lips with his, keeping my hands firmly on either side of his face. I needed to feel the same connection again that we had just shared. I was worried that I had just shown him too much of my broken soul and scared him away.

As my kiss grew hungrier I began to feel him melt back into it. His arm slid underneath me and pulled me closer to his bare chest. My heart beat rapidly as his hand caressed my cheek so tenderly that I found myself fighting back the tears that had been building at the thought of him disconnecting from me. I had fought with myself for so long over the decision to be with him, and now I was worried that I had given too much to him, that he would now consider me disposable and I wouldn't be able to hold on to him. I was desperate to feel the connection we had shared the night before, and to believe that this was not a one-night stand.

As I felt his rapid heartbeat against my bare chest I knew he wanted me as much as I wanted him. I arched my back towards him and wrapped my legs around his hips. I released my hands from his face and ran my nails up his back and through his hair. He groaned in my mouth as I repeated the same motions and felt him grow hard against my inner thigh. I rocked my hips upwards, almost begging him to enter me, eager to feel him inside me. I was well and truly past wanting it—I needed it.

He lifted me upwards before positioning himself with expert precision to enter me without breaking our kiss. I tried to edge my way down the bed, desperate for him to fill me, but he held me so tightly that I struggled to budge even an inch. I felt a cheeky smile creep across his face as my impatience grew and my slick desire became evident as he rubbed the edge of his shaft up and down, spreading my desire along his cock. As he broke away from me I didn't want to open my eyes. I covered my face with my hands out of sheer frustration before he pulled them away, pinning my wrists to the bed. A flutter of panic erupted in my core before he took me by surprise, crushing my lips with his and driving into me with such force my head hit the headboard. I cried out in a mix of ecstasy and pain as he thrust into me deeper and faster with the same smooth motions that threatened an almost instant climax. He then broke away from me again and nuzzled his lips into my neck, kissing and sucking on the tender spot just below my earlobe. I arched my back again as his thrusts became more driven before I felt his body tremble violently above me and we reached climax in unison. As I breathed raggedly I realised right then and there that I was definitely a morning sex person . . . I was an anytime sex person as long as it was with Hugh.

'Holy shit, babe, that was incredible,' he whispered as his heartbeat echoed in his voice and his sentiment echoed in my mind.

We lay there for such a long time that I almost fell asleep in his arms again, curled up in my favourite place—my little nook in between his shoulder and arm—as he kissed my sweat-ridden forehead gently.

After I had showered and dressed I wished that reality and the world outside would disappear and I could stay with him in the apartment forever. My bubble was about to burst, though, as our responsibilities were remembered and I prepared for my work meeting.

I knew that this time it wasn't going to be long until we saw each other. He craved me as much as I craved him; he had shown it in more ways than one and this gave me the confidence to return to reality without fear of when I would see him next. I was not another notch in his belt—I was different.

I walked into the lounge room with my bags and saw him sitting at the table behind his laptop. He looked delectable in his business attire, exuding a level of power and sophistication that turned me on. What had he done to me? I was becoming an animal! I could have stood there all day looking at him.

'What are you looking at?' he said as he raised his eyes from the computer, catching me staring at him.

'The sexiest man to walk this planet,' I responded flirta-tiously, giggling from the inside out. All this giggling was so out of character for me but I was enjoying it.

'Well, you're not too bad yourself,' he said playfully.

I walked towards him, dreading leaving but knowing it was inevitable.

'I have to head off,' I said in a matter-of-fact tone as he stood up to face me.

'When will I see you again?' he asked with a slight hint of longing.

'Soon,' I promised as I wrapped my arms around his neck before he placed his hand on the small of my back, pulled me closer to his body and kissed me softly.

I pulled away slowly, taking in his delicious scent just one more time before he walked me to the door. He kissed me again passionately before I walked over the threshold and said goodbye.

As the elevator arrived and the doors closed in front of me I felt as though my heart had been ripped out of me. The entire way home I cried. I cried for the fact that I was leaving him but also the fact that I had been able to break down my barriers on my own terms. I finally felt like I was freed from the chains of my past. Hugh had come into my life at the right time and now I was able to allow him into my heart without any fear of what it would mean when I returned to my reality without him. My thoughts about what that might be like changed every day as I battled my inner demons, but every now and then I didn't feel as afraid of the consequences. I knew deep down after the night we had spent together that there was no turning back. I was caught up in everything that he promised and the aching in my heart showed me I was capable of letting someone in, even if it was only a little. What the future held I had no idea but right at that point in time I couldn't bear the thought of a future without Hugh Montgomery in it.

#NinthConfession

#COAMMPlaylist:

'Baby, I Love Your Way'

Big Mountain

When I left him I went about my meetings as usual. My days were always full with anything from preparing proposals for my clients, meeting with executives to strategy-building. There was never a moment that I didn't think of Hugh, which at times was distracting. Every now and then flashes of the night before would flood through my mind and catch me by surprise. His lips on my skin, his tender touch and the intoxicating smell of him swirled under my nose as if he was right in front of me. I felt alive for the first time in my life and I didn't mind Hugh intruding into my mind when I was supposed to be concentrating on other tasks. I found myself smiling brightly and had a spring in my step as I thought about how far I had come personally and how far we had come from that very first night. I didn't need to message him and tell him how I was feeling because I had said it all in my actions. It had taken Hugh twelve months to get me into bed, and I was glad I had waited. He was the first person I had ever felt safe enough to share everything with, he was the first person I had ever slept with and I knew deep down that I had made the right decision. Hugh had taught me some incredible things about love, life and patience. I no longer felt the need to panic about where we were headed or what it meant for my future. I was blissfully happy, and nothing was going to ruin that.

Two weeks after we spent our first night together I decided to fly out to see Hugh. The distance was driving me crazy; I wanted to wake up next to him and spend many late nights making love, but I felt like it wasn't possible at that point in time for reasons I couldn't really explain. As the blissful state had begun to wear off I started to wonder if and when it was ever going to be possible to have that kind of relationship . . . and if I even really wanted that.

I texted Hugh to let him know I was on my way.

Flying down tonight, are you free? x I sent with a smile on my face and excitement filling my heart. Although I was confused about what I really wanted, knowing that he was excited to see me always brought a smile to my face.

He seemed over the moon at my impulsive decision. *Absolutely, what time do you land? I'll pick you up. Can't wait to see you. x* he responded.

Pushing the fears to the back of my mind again, I booked myself into a hotel and sped off to the airport for a last-minute flight. I made it just in time after a hectic day at the office. During the flight my nerves were in overdrive: the last time I saw Hugh I had slept with him willingly but highly intoxicated, and I began to panic about whether I would be able to endure it all over again sober with my inhibitions at an all-time high. I feared the wall that had been lowered would shoot back up and if so that would surely set off alarm bells in his head. He would have so many questions and I wouldn't know how to answer them without breaking down or sounding completely nuts. Neither of these scenarios was an option, so I simply had to get a grip.

As soon as I walked out of the airport I looked around the arrivals pick-up and could feel his eyes burning into my flesh. I couldn't spot him but I knew he was there. I spun around and felt my heart race uncontrollably as his eyes connected with mine through the front windscreen. He was sitting in his blacked-out Range Rover, looking straight through me, his dark eyes sending shivers down my spine. There was no turning back; the look in his eyes screamed desire and passion. I blushed as I walked towards him with my gaze focused on the ground. He climbed out of the car and ran to the passenger side to open the door for me. As I looked up to see him standing there I was finally able to take him in. He took my hand gently and placed his free hand on the small of my back before kissing me softly on my right cheek. I felt my neck instinctively arch in the opposite direction to give him access to my neck. I could smell his cologne and feel his touch, his breath on my cheek sending violent currents of electricity crashing down on me from head to toe. As he lifted me up into the car I could feel the air leaving my lungs in a heavy exhale that was almost painful.

The moment he was inside the car he was on me. I was relieved his windows were so heavily tinted as he leaned across the centre console and took my breath away with his kiss. His growing hunger and passion had me melting further and further into the seat. With my eyes shut tightly I began to imagine climbing over the centre console and onto his lap, placing my own hands on either side of his face and kissing him with everything I had inside me. I craved skin-on-skin contact and I imagined ripping his shirt off and running my nails down his chest as his hands ran up and down my back, and then I imagined taking him then and there. As I opened my eyes I knew I was going to be able to defeat the demons inside me—nothing was going to make me take a step back, I was going to continue moving forward, with Hugh.

We drove in silence to the hotel and when we arrived he opened the door for me again and helped me out of the car with the same care as before. He parked the car and carried in my luggage as I checked in and freshened up.

We ordered room service for dinner, which allowed us to sit back and relax in each other's company. I preferred this to spending time out and about in the city. It was selfish, but I wanted him all to myself.

Hugh poured a glass of champagne for us both, and my hands began to shake as I drank it lying on the bed watching football. A few minutes later he took my glass, placed it on the bedside table and then covered my eyes with his warm hands.

'Keep your eyes closed,' he whispered as he took his hands away. My pulse began to race as I heard a small rustle to my right and then felt a small weight placed in front of me.

'Open,' he whispered with a smile in his voice.

As my eyes adjusted to the light I was taken aback by the beautiful pale pink bag with a black bow that was placed in front of me. I was afraid to open it, torn between wanting to know what was inside, and not. When I finally looked inside, I found the most beautiful gifts wrapped up in pink tissue paper. I struggled briefly over whether to accept them. I didn't want anything from him; I cherished what was inside the bag because clearly he had put thought into it but all I ever wanted from him was his love and affection, and I didn't want to set a precedent—he didn't have to buy me things to keep me.

I looked up at him, placing my right hand on his face as I studied his eyes. He had the most incredibly intense brown eyes that bored into my soul. As our gaze intensified I found myself drawing closer to him without even realising it.

His lips locked with mine, my eyes snapped shut immediately and before I knew it I was grasping at his white business shirt, pulling it off him with raw desire. He caressed my skin with gentle kisses as his hands began to explore my body. His breath quickened and I realised he was just as caught up in me as I was in him. He was my drug, something I couldn't give up even if I tried. The passion he exuded was intense and grew with every touch, every glance, every breath and every kiss. There was no escaping it: I was falling madly in love with this man.

He lifted me up, taking off my shirt before gently laying my head down on the pillow as he slid over me, his weight crushing me into the bed. I was nervous and my hands betrayed me as I fumbled trying to unbutton his pants. He began to laugh as I grew frustrated. I was fighting not only to get the pants off him but also to quiet the voice in my head that was telling me that I was entering dangerous territory.

After he removed his pants I was itching to feel him inside me. I ran my nails down his back, clawing at his skin with animal instinct. I felt my pulse racing as he began to slowly take off my jeans. I felt like screaming as my patience began to thin. I arched my back as he ripped off my jeans and G-string in one swift motion.

In an instant he was back on top of me, lightly kissing the tender spot on my neck. I was desperate to flip him over and take control, but he was taking thing agonisingly slowly.

I wrapped my legs around his waist and tried to pull him down closer to me. He laughed, knowing he was teasing me. Well, two can play at this game, I thought to myself.

I waited for him to begin his descent of kisses down my chest and towards my stomach before I slipped out of his grip and pummelled him to the bed before he had a chance to realise what was happening. He looked up at me blankly as I straddled him and grabbed his wrists, pinning them down on the bed before he could protest. I crushed my mouth to his and caressed his tongue with mine. The control and power made my fears evaporate; I was able to determine the pace. I gave him a wicked smile as I broke away, still keeping his hands pinned to the bed.

'Well, now you have me, what are you going to do with me, dear Ava?' He raised his eyebrows and returned my smile.

'I have a few ideas,' I said, mulling over which one to put into action first. 'I've got you right where I want you, Mr Montgomery. Now, close your eyes and don't move your arms or you will be in trouble,' I warned.

He didn't protest and did just as I asked. I looked at him for a moment with his eyes closed; he looked so peaceful and at ease with me. I felt myself taking a breath in as I began my descent of kisses along his chest, replicating his own methods to determine the reaction I would get. I ran my nails lightly down his chest until my trail finally led me to his cock. Just as I placed my hand on the rigid length of him, he flipped me over and pinned my hands above my head.

'You didn't think you'd get away with it that easily, did you?' he whispered, kissing my neck again.

'No fair!' I squealed, trying playfully—and unsuccessfully—to pull my wrists out from his grip. I could feel him at my opening and was desperate to move a little lower to feel him enter me. At that very moment I would have given anything to feel it.

'This isn't about me, Ava, it's about you. Be patient,' he whispered.

He made his way down my neck again, this time leaving trails of wet kisses. My pulse quickened as he rolled his hips around me. I exhaled as I moved my hips in unison with his. He finally reached my chest and placed his lips around the tip of my nipple before taking it whole into his mouth at the same time that he unexpectedly drove into me so hard I let out a moan in delight.

He sucked harder, running his teeth lightly along the edge of my nipple as he continued thrusting into me deeper and deeper. I arched my back, desperate to feel him fill me. He removed his hands from my wrists and slipped them underneath me. I tightened my legs around his waist and ran my hands through his hair as he picked up his pace.

I felt my climax building but I was desperate to hold out to feel him in me for longer. He massaged my breasts in such a way that had me teetering on the edge of a brutal orgasm. Moans of delight escaped my mouth before I had the chance to silence them as he reached up and grabbed my hair, pulling it gently, exposing my neck and running kisses up it until he reached my mouth and kissed me gently. With one arm underneath me and a hand on my face he whispered to me, looking me straight in the eyes with such an intense gaze I almost climaxed, as his eyes showed me something I wasn't prepared to see.

'Come now, Ava,' he whispered quietly, and as if on cue, I did. The ripples of fire that erupted around my body left me feeling euphoric. Spasms shook me so uncontrollably around his length that I didn't realise he had begun to climax at the same time. I was milking him dry and yet he couldn't get enough of thrusting into me. Before I knew it I was climaxing again, the smell of sex in the air mixed with his cologne, the sound of his voice as he came and the continued thrusts sending me over the edge. The second climax had me stifling a scream; it was so powerful that my eyes filled with stars as my vision blackened, my body filled with pins and needles as I lost myself in the moment. I kissed him ferociously as I took him whole once more.

With him still inside me I rolled him onto his back and ran kisses all over his body. The ripples of pleasure were dulling slightly as my aching sex squeezed against his throbbing cock once more. He moaned again before running his hands down my back ever so lightly, making goose bumps erupt all over me.

As I lay in his arms I began to drift off. I was spent and just wanted to fall asleep in his arms again and stay in this position forever . . . but I knew he had to leave as he had a meeting early in the morning on the other side of town. It was only when I thought about this that it hit me: he might be going home to someone else. I pushed the ugly thoughts to the back of my mind and negotiated with my conscience, deciding I would deal with that at another time. Right now I was going to enjoy the moment.

'Ava, you are incredible, that was incredible. I feel so alive,' he whispered, kissing my forehead. I couldn't respond—I was afraid that if I did I would end up saying something I would regret—so instead I relaxed my body and pretended to fall asleep. Soon after that I did.

I don't know how much later it was that I woke up to him standing beside the bed fully dressed, pulling up the covers around me and kissing my forehead and cheeks.

I was exhausted but I mustered the strength to pull him towards me as he began to pull away. He sat beside me and leaned down towards me, laying me back on the pillow without breaking our tender kiss. He was so gentle with me, it always made me melt inside.

'Ava, please don't make this hard. I don't want to leave but I have to,' he whispered into my ear.

'It's fine, I understand,' I replied, not knowing what it was that I was supposed to be understanding but I was too tired to argue and didn't want to ruin the moment.

'Sleep well, beautiful. I'll call you in the morning,' he said, tucking strands of my hair gently behind my ear and kissing me once more before he left and I fell asleep.

•

The next morning my body ached all over. Standing in the steaming hot shower, I could still feel him on me, in me and all over me. I didn't want to wash the memories away but I needed to hit the gym. Twenty minutes later I stepped out of the shower and looked at my reflection in the mirror. As I pulled my hair back I noticed a glow about me that I had never seen before. I was in the best mood possible and was so excited for the day ahead.

Once I reached the gym I headed for the rowing machine. I was the only person there and watched as my mind's eye replayed the night before. My blissful mood was interrupted by my phone ringing—it was Hugh. At that exact moment the memory of him leaving hit me with full force. It was then that his words filled my head and I realised that I was officially the other woman. I let the call go to voicemail as I sat on the rowing machine, my conscience taking over and bringing tears to my eyes. What happened when he returned home? Was his wife there? Did he sleep in her bed? How did I really feel about that? It struck me that I may have to share the only person I had ever loved.

My good mood disintegrated and I returned to my room, where I stayed for the rest of the day. I refused to answer my phone and didn't want to do anything but watch movies and sleep. After a few hours I saw his name pop up on the caller ID again. I picked up my phone and threw it against the wall. I watched as it fell to the ground, the tears coming again as it continued to ring. Not long after that I fell asleep watching a movie.

When I awoke an hour later I picked up my phone and saw two missed calls and five messages. I felt sick at the thought of opening them, so I ran myself a bath, sitting on the cold tiles wrapped in only a towel. I heard the running water filling the bath and felt the hot tears stream down my face as I read each of his messages.

Thank you for such a wonderful night, beautiful.

Are you okay? What are you doing tonight?

Ava?

Are you still at the hotel? I want to see you.

If you don't call me back immediately I will turn this car around. Call me.

The only response I could muster was *I'm fine* before I watched my phone fall out of my hand and fall to the floor. I stood, dropped my towel on the tiles and stepped into the steaming bath filled with lavender. As I slipped my head under the water I could feel the humiliation washing all over my body. I felt the pain in my heart grow as my mind kept repeating the same insulting sentence: 'I told you so.'

I was in so deep, I didn't know how I was going to walk away unscathed. I felt like it was the beginning of the end but little did I realise that it was only the start of one hectic rollercoaster ride.

#TenthConfession

#COAMMPlaylist:

'Killing Me Softly'

Colbie Caillat

I didn't return Hugh's calls or messages for the rest of my trip. I needed space and I couldn't tell him why. I knew I would push him away if I responded with everything that was running through my head, so I chose to stay silent.

When I finally returned home I found myself going over everything he had said and done, trying to figure out what was happening between us. I was driving myself crazy. I had never fallen in love with someone before and the person I had chosen turned out to be completely unavailable—well, to the best of my knowledge. He had never actually confirmed that he was still with his wife, but his not staying the night when I was in town had me suspicious. What confused me the most was that he was so open about us and it was quite obvious to anyone he knew around us that there was something more than friendship there. Despite my confusion, though, I had never found the courage to just ask him. The next time I saw Hugh I was determined to talk about it; I needed clarity and I had to know what I was getting myself into. It turned out, though, that the next time I saw him would be under incredibly bad circumstances.

One morning as I sat in my office working on a contract my phone rang. I didn't recognise the number and decided I would take the call outside. Something inside me told me that it was best to have some privacy.

'Hello,' I answered.

'Hello, is this Ava Reilly?' said a male voice.

'Speaking,' I confirmed.

The caller identified himself as a detective from an interstate police commission and told me he wanted to discuss Hugh. My heart sank and I struggled to breathe, let alone respond—I knew this couldn't be good.

When I asked what it was regarding I heard words that left me speechless.

'I would like to discuss with you a pending legal case against Mr Montgomery in which we believe you have information that will support the current allegations.' I was gobsmacked. What the hell did that mean? And what could I possibly know?

The detective went on to specify a text message that had been sent to me. I knew the message he was talking about but I had no idea of its relevance, as the context of the conversation was a joke that Hugh and I had shared. He began to explain the allegations and I was caught off guard. I had nothing to do with anything he was suggesting, and indeed I couldn't see how the message had anything to do with anything.

'Detective Warwick, I don't know anything about any of these allegations,' I said. 'I don't know anything about Mr Montgomery's business affairs. We work closely but not that closely.'

'Would it be fair to say that there is a personal relationship between you and Mr Montgomery?' he asked in a smug tone.

I took a breath and replied as calmly as I could: 'We are friends, close friends, but I'm not sure what that has to do with anything, I don't know anything about what you have told me. I'm sorry but I can't help you any further.'

He then had the nerve to tell me he didn't believe me. He said he would give me twenty-four hours to 'think about it' and then he would call me back. And in the meantime I wasn't to say anything to Hugh.

Within seconds of ending the call I spoke with my boss. She called Hugh but reached his voicemail. She told him to call her immediately but didn't say why.

When he called me minutes later I told him everything in a state of panic. He tried to calm me but I screamed at him, demanding to know why he had involved me in this. He told me that I wasn't the only one who had received such a call and that the police were trying to tear his life apart. He swore he hadn't done anything wrong and I truly believed in his innocence. During the call we heard a *click-click* sound, which Hugh explained meant our phones were tapped. Within seconds of getting off the phone he texted me from another mobile and we began to communicate via that number.

As promised the next day the detective called, and I reiterated that I knew nothing.

'I don't believe you,' he said, echoing his comments from the previous day. 'How could you *not* know? My partner and I would like to fly up to interview you.' I knew he wouldn't stop until I met with him, so I set a time the following day and prepared myself to tell him exactly what I had already said a million times: I knew nothing.

I wasn't scared when they arrived the next day but I was very naive—I didn't even ask to see their identification. Mostly I was worried about what might happen to Hugh.

We met at a coffee shop around the corner from my office. During the interview I found out a lot of new information about Hugh and his family, and it was clear that the officers still didn't believe that I didn't know anything.

'Ms Reilly, we know you know *something*. We will pick you up from your office this afternoon and take your official statement. Once we have that, you can return to your life as it is.'

'If I give my statement can you guarantee that I will not be subpoenaed and this will be the end of it all?' I said hopefully.

'Absolutely. Once you have made your statement, that's it,' he replied in a soothing voice.

'Fine,' I responded reluctantly. By the end of their trip they would know they had wasted their time.

That afternoon they picked me up from the office. As we drove they told me all sorts of terrible things about Hugh— basically that he was the scum of the earth. Clearly they were trying to rattle me, and I tried my hardest to ignore everything they said. It wasn't until I had been in the car with them for twenty minutes that they told me they were taking me to the motel where they were staying. Alarm bells immediately rang in my head and I began to silently hyperventilate. I contemplated jumping out of the car while it was moving, but I was frozen to the seat. As we turned the corner I saw the motel: it was dirty, and the thought of going in sent spirals of fear through me. I didn't know what was going to happen but I immediately feared the worst. I said a prayer that I would be able to walk out of this situation alive. After everything I had been through, this couldn't be the end.

#EleventhConfession

#COAMMPlaylist:

'Kissing You'

Des'ree

As we entered the motel I saw a man shooting drugs into his arm in the park across the road. I felt trapped, and terrified. We walked the flights of stairs and entered the officers' room, where they explained that they couldn't take me to a police station because they needed to keep our meeting private. They locked the door and told me to sit down at the table, where they opened the laptop and asked for my details. Despite my fear and confusion I could feel that this was about to become a good-cop–bad-cop routine, and I was determined to tell the truth: that I knew nothing.

The detectives still didn't believe me, and they were annoyed when I told them I needed to make a phone call. As soon as I got out of the room I ran down the hall as quickly as I could and almost tripped down the stairs. When I burst through the front doors I collapsed against a brick wall and called Hugh. I couldn't tell him where I was or the predicament I was in but I went off at him anyway. I yelled at him, telling him how horrified I was and that I couldn't believe I had been dragged into his mess, especially when I didn't know anything. He apologised profusely but I couldn't take in another word. I hung up as my mother called me, and after I told her what was happening my father called emergency services. He repeated their instructions to me: stay put and under no circumstances should I go anywhere else with the two detectives. Legally they had to tell the local authorities that they were interstate, but they hadn't done this, which made the whole episode feel even stranger. Seconds after I hung up from my mother, emergency services called me and told me they were sending local police officers to check on me, and that I should stay on the phone with them until that happened.

In the worst possible timing, my phone cut out as one of the detectives came downstairs and told me to come back to the room with him.

My mother called me back and began to scream at me not to go near him as the detective demanded I get back upstairs. I was utterly confused and panicked.

'Ava, if you do not come back upstairs and finish your statement, then this is going to get much worse. We can do this the easy way or the hard way!' he shouted.

'I'm not coming back up with you. I told you I don't know anything,' I said as I tried to tune out my mother's panicked voice in my ear.

The detective glared at me. 'Fine, have it your way. Stay here. You've chosen the hard way,' he spat before turning around and running upstairs.

I lit a cigarette and forced myself not to cry. Within a minute the detectives returned with their diaries and stern looks on their face.

The first detective handed me a piece of paper that was a summons to a secret hearing. He told me rudely that I was not allowed to tell anyone other than my employer and legal counsel about the summons or the hearing—and he emphasised that I was not allowed to discuss it with Hugh. He advised me that if I didn't turn up to the hearing a warrant would be issued for my arrest.

'But I really don't know anything!' I said.

'Bullshit!' he swore before reading me rights and leaving me there alone.

I collapsed against the brick wall again as the local police arrived. They examined the summons and told me that indeed I had to attend the hearing or I would be arrested. I felt my throat close up in that moment as the reality of the situation caught up with me.

After taking my statement, the local officers went to find the detectives and verify their identities. When I took a closer look at the documents I saw that they had been sent at 1 p.m. that day, before I had met up with the detectives; clearly they had planned all along to give me the summons.

Just before I left, one of the detectives approached me and said something that will always stay with me.

'We know you know something, and we *will* find out what it is. Pillow talk talks—don't be stupid thinking you're the only one.' Before I had the chance to respond he walked off.

I was left standing alone with the police car lights flashing around me. Suddenly I felt like getting involved with Hugh was the biggest mistake of my life. He couldn't help me; I was in this alone. No one could protect me.

I felt like I was playing Russian roulette without knowing the stakes. My sanity? My life as I knew it? The only person I had ever truly loved?

How was I going to get through this alone?

#TwelfthConfession

#COAMMPlaylist:

'Feels Like Home'

Chantal Kreviazuk

The night before I was due to fly out for the hearing, I lay in bed awake until well after one o'clock. Even though I had a flight at seven-thirty—after landing at nine-thirty I would then have to race into the city for the ten o'clock hearing—I couldn't relax enough to fall asleep.

Adding to my stress was the fact that I woke up late and almost missed my flight. As I made my way through the skies I tried to keep panic at bay by focusing on my lawyer's words. I had chosen not to have legal representation in court as I was only being called as a witness. Under any other circumstances I would have wanted a lawyer with me on the day, but I knew I didn't have anything to be worried about when it came to my lack of involvement.

'Don't go into the personal relationship with Hugh. If they try to talk about it, then object and ask what the relevance is. Remember, the judge isn't actually on your side. This is a secret hearing and it isn't like a normal court case. The judge and counsel want to find a way to nail Hugh. Be honest and remember that you need to protect yourself.'

The only thing I wanted to do was protect Hugh but I had no idea what I was protecting him from. As I walked through the terminal I looked around at the people passing by and for the first time I thought about how complicated my life had seemed to become since I met Hugh. I hadn't asked for this, and there was a chance it could ruin my career prospects but I really didn't care. What I *did* care for was Hugh—so much that no matter what happened, it all seemed worth it.

It had been a week since the detectives interviewed me, and in that time the media had jumped on the case and decided to paint Hugh as the villain. These vultures knew that good guys don't sell newspapers, but the image they were presenting to the public was nothing like the person I knew Hugh to be. The so-called facts that they kept reporting were far from the truth, and because Hugh was a very private person they could only manage to report the same story over and over again with rarely any new developments.

As the cab pulled up outside the courthouse I felt a wave of relief to not see any reporters. I had no idea who knew about this hearing but what I did know was that leaks happened all the time and I couldn't afford to have my face or name attached to a case that had been splashed over all the media in every corner of Australia, especially considering I had a personal relationship with the primary person of interest. Over the past week I had kept my distance from Hugh but there was no way we could cut all contact, so we made sure that we only communicated through a number that was not associated with him. We didn't talk about the court case in any detail and it was only through television and newspaper reports that I had seen Hugh turning himself in when charges were officially laid. I saw the detectives raiding his office for computers, phones and any anything else they could get their hands on. It seemed so invasive and made me feel even more protective towards him.

As I pushed through the second set of glass doors I was faced with an X-ray machine and armed federal police officers. I felt like a criminal even though I knew I hadn't done anything wrong. My hands trembled and tears welled in my eyes as the enormity of the situation hit me in full force: this was real. I couldn't stop myself from panicking at the thought that Hugh could go to jail for something that in my heart I didn't think he had any part in.

Passing through the final security doors and signing in, I felt like everything was in slow motion. Armed police officers and officials passed me in groups of two as I was asked to sit and wait. My nerves ramped up in anticipation of the unknown. I had spoken to police prosecutors all week and yet they really hadn't prepared me mentally for what I had to face. I was so young, and I had no idea that any word I spoke could be used against me in court. Luckily, I might have been young but I wasn't naive. I planned on making sure that I thought about everything carefully before I allowed anything to come out of my mouth. I wasn't going to be a part of the hanging committee for someone I personally deemed to be innocent.

Twenty minutes later I was escorted through two large oak doors and into a wide open space that had a row of wooden pews, a long desk occupied by four people with their computers at the ready, a judge sitting high up at a raised desk, and directly opposite him another desk, which I was motioned to sit at. The room was empty apart from the officials, making it truly feel like a secret hearing. I seemed to be the only person set to take the stand.

A few minutes later I was instructed by the judge that I had to take an oath, and it was then that I had to make a choice: would I do anything to protect Hugh, or would I tell the complete truth regardless of the consequences?

As I uttered the oath I knew in my heart that I would tell the whole truth, no matter what it cost me. I suddenly felt that regardless of what I said that day my words would end up being used against Hugh, and I instantly felt guilty. I decided that although I might not be capable of lying I was going to make sure that I chose my words carefully, to spare him as much pain as possible.

In the beginning I was made to feel at ease with simple questions about my knowledge of the events that had transpired and whether I had any involvement in them. All I really knew was what the media had reported to have happened but I wasn't one to get involved in salacious gossip or even believe it for that matter. I knew in this industry that if you were in the public eye the media would paint you in one of two lights, a victim or a villain, and they were making damn sure that Hugh was painted as a villain. These questions lulled me into a false sense of security because they made me think the prosecutors were beginning to realise that I really didn't know anything. The rug was pulled firmly out from underneath me, however, when the prosecutor began to ask me very personal questions about Hugh and our relationship. My lawyer's words echoed in my head as I objected profusely to the line of questioning. Fortunately the judge agreed and I wasn't forced to answer the questions. The prosecutor seemed pissed off at not being able to pull a fast one on either of us, and he quickly changed tactic and asked in a very roundabout way the same questions he had tried to ask before—and this time I was forced to answer.

I reiterated that I knew nothing about Hugh's business dealings, and this became even more evident as their questions repeatedly ended in the same answers. Just as I thought that the truth of my statements was sinking in, they decided it was time to pull the ace from their sleeve to top off an already shitty day.

'Ava, we would like to discuss a text message that you received from Mr Montgomery on the day in question,' said the pissed-off prosecutor. I looked at him blankly. Surely we had covered this already? How many more ways could he ask me what it had meant?

'Yes,' I responded frostily. This was going round and round in circles and he was no longer the only one who was angry. He looked away from me with a smile on his face and turned to the judge.

'We would like to take Ms Reilly's phone to have our technical analysts try to retrieve a copy of the information we believe is relevant to this case and any information that may have been deleted.'

I was floored. They couldn't just take my phone—it was my business and my lifeline to Hugh. I wasn't going to let them win without a fight. My flight was only three hours away and what they were proposing would mean that I would be leaving the state without my phone.

'I object,' I said coolly, looking the judge directly in the eye. 'They already have copies of my text messages, as is evident by their line of questioning. I cannot leave without my phone; it would cost me quite a lot of business.'

Judging by the expression on the prosecutor's face—his eyes and mouth were wide open—he hadn't expected this response from me.

'Noted, Ms Reilly,' replied the judge. 'We will take a short recess to discuss the options and will return in one hour.'

Once I walked outside I knew that I should eat something but my stomach was doing backflips. Despite feeling ill I lit up a cigarette and felt the nicotine immediately calm me. With shaking hands I pulled out my phone and dialled Hugh's private number.

'Hey, baby, how are you?' he answered with such a delightfully soothing tone I almost collapsed on the street. I desperately wanted to tell him everything but knew that legally I couldn't. I needed to see him, to feel safely wrapped in his arms even if it was only for a little while.

'I'm okay. I'm in town actually. What are you up to?' I tried to keep my voice calm, but he didn't miss anything, and he knew that something was up almost as soon as the words left my mouth.

'Ava, where are you?' he said with determination saturating his voice.

'I'm in the city. I'm just on a quick break and I fly out this afternoon. Are you around at all?' I asked, hoping he was close enough that I could zip away and just see him for even five minutes.

'I'm on my way to a meeting in the northern suburbs. Ava, how long are you here for?' I could hear the concern in his voice. We both knew that I would never come to town without telling him first, and I was glad that he knew to play the conversation game wisely enough that anyone listening wouldn't pick up on the unspoken words we were exchanging. Hugh knew that I wasn't being transparent. I don't know how we had managed to figure out our own little language without even speaking to each other but for some reason I felt like he knew why I was there and wasn't pressing me for any further detail over the phone.

'I leave at four this afternoon,' I said as confidently as possible.

'Can you reschedule your flight? I really want to see you.' I knew what he was asking, and it wasn't just about changing flights.

'I can't, Hugh. I'll be back soon, unless you plan to fly into town any time soon?' I said, hoping I had given him enough to work with, without actually saying anything about why I was really there and why the time constraint.

'I will. I promise.' The sadness echoed down the phone.

I knew he understood exactly what I was going through and he was devastated that he couldn't be there for me.

We hung up a short time later and when I looked at my phone I realised the hour was nearly up. I returned to the courthouse and was called in almost immediately.

I took the stand again and was informed that the judge had granted the prosecutors the ability to take my phone and retrieve what they could but only in relation to Hugh. In return for my cooperation I would be provided with a loan phone and accommodation in town for the night while they retrieved what they needed to. I knew immediately what it was that I wanted to do with my spare time—I knew I had to see Hugh. I had to gauge what was going on in his head and a little part of me wanted to see if anything they had said was true.

I was strongly advised not to see Hugh, but their advice was not something I was prepared to take. They may have commandeered my phone but I wasn't about to let them tell me with whom I could spend time.

An hour later I checked into the hotel and once safely in the room I called my lawyer. He told me that under no circumstances was I to let Hugh into my room, because it could be bugged. He also stressed that the temporary phone I had been given was surely bugged, so I shouldn't take it out with me or talk with Hugh on it about anything.

I was definitely going to take *his* advice, but I was also going to get to the bottom of this with Hugh one way or another.

I called Hugh and told him that my phone was in for repair and that I had a temporary one. I made sure to keep the phone calls short and sweet and made sure that all text messages were cryptic: Hugh would know exactly what I was saying but it would take anyone else a while to figure it out. We agreed to meet for dinner that night, and after the stress of my day I began to really looking forward to it.

Because I wasn't expecting to stay overnight I hadn't packed any clothes and so later that afternoon I went shopping to pick something out. I chose a black cardigan and an orange maxi dress, and when I got ready for dinner I let my jet-black hair flow down onto it.

A few hours later I went down to the lobby, leaving my phone in the room as instructed. I felt so relaxed and surprisingly at ease without a phone. I felt free and finally able to talk to Hugh without worrying about anyone else hearing our words.

As I walked out of the hotel towards Hugh's car I felt the familiar electricity burn up and down my spine. I couldn't believe where I was or the situation I was in but in that moment none of it mattered. As he approached me I realised that just looking into his eyes, feeling his touch as he placed his hand on the small of my back or the safety I felt in his presence was worth every moment of pain I was feeling. He had changed my life, broken down my walls, and in that instant all the worry left my mind and body. He was exactly what I needed.

We drove to the restaurant in silence. He had not let go of my hand from the moment we got into the car and as I gazed out the window at the beautiful night sky he squeezed my fingers. I looked towards him and felt his eyes lock with mine. I glanced away immediately, afraid that he would see past the front and deep inside my soul, which was hiding one of the biggest secrets I had ever been forced to keep.

Dinner was incredibly rich in experience and flavour. I had never had Indian food before, so during the courses Hugh made me close my eyes and fed me some of the most delicious food that I had ever tasted. He said he wanted me to experience every flavour the only way you should ever try something new: blind.

Despite our closeness, our conversation was stiff, and I felt like a fraud not being able to share with him everything that I had learned that day. He asked a few questions about why I was in town and why the sudden change in my plans to stay. I answered the most honest way I could—I told him that I wasn't going to lie, so he shouldn't ask me any more questions. I told him that I was there because I had to be and that was all he needed to know. I knew it was killing him that we couldn't just discuss everything, but he didn't ask again.

I felt so close to him and yet so far away. I didn't want the night to end and I needed to feel his arms around me, have him inside me, connecting with me, because the distance was breaking my heart. I knew, though, that this couldn't happen—not this night.

When we arrived back at the hotel he placed his hand on my chin and kissed me with such force and passion that it knocked the wind out of me. When he pulled back he ran his thumb across my jaw, and I knew what he was saying without him uttering a word. He said it all with his eyes.

I reluctantly moved to climb out of the car but he tugged on my hand to bring me back to him.

'Ava,' he said quietly. 'I understand. It doesn't change a thing and it will never change the way I feel.' He ran his thumb across my knuckles and my throat began to burn. I wanted to scream, I wanted to tell him the truth but I knew I couldn't. I nodded and turned again to leave. My hand slipped from his grip and at the same time it felt as though my heart was being ripped from my chest.

That night in my room I couldn't stop the tears. It seemed as though I was never going to be allowed to be happy. I kept asking myself if it was karma for everything that I had ever done wrong. Was I never going to be able to breathe deeply and calmly, knowing I was safe?

#ThirteenthConfession

#COAMMPlaylist
'Breakeven'
The Script

The next morning I woke up to find myself praying for it all to be over. I dragged myself out of bed and had a shower, but not even standing under the hot water could break down the anxiety that had built up over a restless night.

When I arrived at the courthouse I had no idea what was going to happen; all I knew was that I wanted my phone back and to return to reality. I walked in and sat down, waiting for someone to return my phone so I could go home. I was a mess inside but I managed to remain composed enough to stop myself from fidgeting. Thirty minutes later a woman approached and told me that they had not been successful in obtaining the information they required. Apparently my phone had crashed their systems multiple times and they needed to keep it until they got what they needed. I knew it was horseshit, but what could I do?

I argued with her for what felt like an eternity, and after talking with the judge she returned with a court order to say that she could keep my phone and that it would be mailed back to me. This was the final straw, and I burst into tears. I wasn't crying over the phone, I was just exhausted and really wanted it all to be over.

The entire flight home I found myself slipping into a low state. As soon as I landed I arranged to meet with my lawyer to debrief about the trip.

As I sat in his city-view office finishing the story of what had happened he leaned back in his chair behind his mahogany desk and soaked up every sordid detail from the motel room to the court case.

After a few moments of silence as he watched me carefully and clearly thought about his next words. 'What the police did,' he began, 'taking you to that motel, is a serious offence. We have a number of options. We can go after them for the severe stress it has obviously caused you. Or . . .' He paused and took in a deep breath, which made me feel very uncomfortable. I was desperate for him to spit it out!

'The conduct of the detectives while here in town is extremely questionable. It could be the very thing that gets this case thrown out.' He then went on to tell me that because of their questionable interrogation techniques, the detectives who interviewed me might also have behaved inappropriately with other witnesses, which might cast enough doubt over how other testimonies were taken to pull apart the case against Hugh.

'If you were to seek legal advice from a lawyer in that state, you would not be in violation of your court order . . . and if it happened to be the same lawyer employed by Hugh, well, that would just be a coincidence.'

I took in every word he said, all the while desperately hoping that it might just work.

As soon as I left the office I called Hugh's lawyer and left him a message asking him to call me back. Three days later I still hadn't heard from him and I was starting to get nervous. Couldn't he see that this was urgent and that I could help with this case?

I called Hugh on his new mobile number and asked him how I could contact his lawyer. I didn't say why, but he knew. Less than ten minutes later the lawyer called me and immediately rubbed me up the wrong way. He advised me that he was recording the conversation, which made me very uncomfortable. He then proceeded to tell me that I was not allowed to tell him if I had been involved in a secret hearing—in fact I was not allowed to say anything. I agreed that I would avoid specifics before I began to tell my story.

I felt like I was on trial when he began to ask me about my personal relationship with Hugh. I kept tight-lipped, refusing to say anything other than we were close friends. When he asked me if I had ever slept with Hugh, I denied it. I didn't know why he was asking me these questions but my instinct was to play my cards close to my chest and protect Hugh, so I lied.

When we hung up I felt no clearer about what I was going to do. I felt disconnected from myself and afraid of what the future held.

Hugh and I couldn't spend more than a few minutes on the phone, and I felt a distance grow between us. Every day I found myself having to search online for updates on his case, and I hated not being able to discuss it with him or see him.

A few days later as I dressed for the day I felt that something was off. I couldn't explain my nerves, but I found myself typing his name into the search engine. The first article that appeared sent me into a spin. As I read it my heart sank. The article stated that Hugh had been followed by paparazzi to his home the night before; the article included a photograph of his house, which I instantly recognised as the home he owned with his wife.

My mind went into overdrive as I continued to read. The journalist had tried to contact Hugh the following morning at the same house for comment, but Hugh had advised he wouldn't talk, because he was spending time with his family.

I struggled to catch my breath. I couldn't understand what he was doing back there. He was sleeping in that house? Did that mean he was back with her? Did it mean that they were never separated and he had lied?

I was desperate to know the truth but also scared to find out the meaning behind it all. I couldn't bring myself to ask him—I was afraid of hearing something I didn't like, or worse, becoming needy and clingy in his eyes, everything that he despised, so instead I just beat myself up. I couldn't bear the thought of losing him but could I really stay with a man who so obviously had gone back to his wife?

I was so confused and yet I didn't have the courage to find out what the hell was going on. I prepared myself for the worst: that I would have to say goodbye either way . . . it was time to accept that this was the end for Hugh and me.

#FourteenthConfession

#COAMMPlaylist
'California King Bed'
Arlene Zelina

It took me a while to digest the information about Hugh being back in that house. I made my mind up that the next time I was face to face with him I would bring it up. I didn't want to add more stress to his life with everything that was going on, but I knew I couldn't maintain the fantasy that things were okay when they were far from it. I needed to look him in the eye and ask for the truth, and I didn't trust myself not to just accept whatever he would say over the phone. Unless we were together I wouldn't find the courage to ask the questions my heart needed answers to. I continued to speak with him over the phone on a regular basis and each time I bit my tongue as long as I could until I almost couldn't bear it anymore.

After I had spoken to his solicitor I called Hugh and relayed our conversation. I told him that if his lawyer was smart he would take my statement to the courts and fight the validity of the police interrogation not just with me but with any other witnesses. Hugh disagreed, and I didn't fight him on it. He was the only person who could make the decisions about his defence.

I flew down to see him around two weeks after our conversation, and as usual as soon as I stepped out of the airport I felt his presence. As I began to walk towards him I noticed a reporter in the far corner with his camera at the ready. I motioned for Hugh to stay in the car and jumped in just as the photographer began to snap away. It made me very uncomfortable, and it was just my good luck that the photos never hit the media.

We went through our usual routine of silence during the drive to the hotel, and I went to check in while he parked the car and brought up my luggage.

Neither of us spoke about the possibility of leaving the hotel room and we agreed to order in. I knew he was aware that something was wrong—I had barely said more than a few words to him since he had picked me up—but I still couldn't find the courage to discuss what was going on.

After dinner we sat in the suite in deafening silence. I felt my nerves climbing as each second passed, and I could feel the moment approaching . . . the moment that would determine my future with Hugh.

In my haze of thoughts and distraction I didn't notice him get up from the couch, but suddenly he was standing in front of me. He placed his right hand over mine, lifted my chin with his left hand and looked straight into my heart. I saw the pain in his eyes. I found myself holding my breath before swallowing hard to moisten the burning dryness in my throat. I was suddenly terrified, and I knew I couldn't do it to him right then and there. I wanted to hold him, I wanted to protect him and I knew deep down I was going to regret not talking to him, but my natural instinct was to look after him, make him forget the pain of everything that was going on around him and just let him breathe easily around me. I wanted to be the rock in his life, someone he never needed to worry about. The stress of the court case was getting to him: he looked older, had lost weight and looked like he hadn't slept in weeks. I pushed my questions to the back of my mind and decided to let it go for now.

As he brushed his hand down my face to my neck I felt the searing desire growing in the pit of my stomach, and my breath began to hitch as his hands reached my waist and he lifted me from the sofa. He placed his knee strategically between my legs and lifted me so my legs could wrap around him.

Neither of us broke our intense gaze and I could feel the power of his eyes burning into my soul. I blushed as the hunger and roaring passion ignited again between us, and I wrapped my arms around his neck as he walked towards the bedroom. He leaned forward and kissed me before we collapsed onto the bed.

I opened my eyes to look at the man who haunted me. I knew it was irrational and stupid to have fallen for a married man but I found it so hard to let him go. The thought of staying with him was eating at me but the thought of leaving him was like a knife tearing my heart apart so savagely that I knew I wouldn't survive it.

As I looked into his eyes and stopped kissing him I knew we both understood that there were words I needed to say but couldn't. He ran his fingers through my hair as a single tear slid down my right cheek. He placed his thumb gently under my eye to wipe away the tear, then sighed and took in a deep breath before pulling away and running his hand through his hair. He looked so torn up.

I pulled myself up on my elbows and grabbed the back of his neck to kiss him hard, so passionately that I caught him by surprise. I felt the yearning to be with him return and I knew I couldn't share my fears about his wife with him this time. I didn't want him to lie to me, and in my heart I believed that he would—that was the one thing that would see me walk out the door.

I stopped momentarily and pulled my shirt up over my head before returning to kiss him again, this time so gently that I melted into the bed. Even with my eyes closed I knew his body so well. My hands trailed down his shirt, unbuttoning it as quickly as I could but it didn't feel fast enough.

As soon as his bare chest touched my skin I felt a surge of electricity flow from head to toe. I ran my nails down his back and my heart raced as he lifted me up and gently moved me to the head of the bed.

He traced his finger along my cheek as he looked into my eyes. His breath was heavy against my neck and began to drive me crazy. I needed him more than ever. If only the world could have swallowed us up in that moment.

We made love slowly and with such desire to be closer to each other that my heart ached. I wanted him and I needed him like the air that filled my lungs. Each time he entered me I could feel his love coursing through me as he refused to break his piercing gaze into my eyes. I fell harder and faster for him as we made love multiple times. Our appetite for each other was insatiable; each time either of us climaxed it never seemed enough, but by the sixth time I was spent.

I collapsed and curled up against his chest as the pleasure of the final climax began to subside and my breathing slowed. As close as I felt to him, the insecurity began to creep through my blissful state and I knew that I needed to say something.

I pulled myself up onto my elbow and drank in his peaceful face. He stared at me with the same look in his eyes: pure torment. I opened my mouth and before I could stop myself words began to escape.

'I need to know, Hugh . . . Why are you living back in that house? Are you back with her?'

A million things raced through my mind as he exhaled violently and shook his head.

'Ava, I can't do this right now,' he whispered. His voice was full of shame as he climbed out of bed and quickly dressed.

My eyes burned with tears of fury as I felt him clamming up. I was losing him.

'Hugh, I really need to know. I can't be the other woman. I can't do this if that's all I mean,' I said carefully.

He stopped to soak in my words as they echoed around us. You could have cut the tension with a knife. He turned slowly to face me, the tension high as pain flashed across his face.

I felt so vulnerable. I pulled the sheet closer to my chest and sat up, leaning against the headboard as the tears began to sting my eyes and stain my cheeks.

He moved towards me cautiously but I pulled away from him. This time I was the one putting up walls in self-preservation.

He took my hand and rubbed his thumb across my knuckles.

'Ava, I'm not with her. I told you where we stood. I need to be in that house, I need to be there to show a united front. It's not common knowledge that we aren't together, and I don't want this case to hurt my family any more than it has to. I have my children to think about, and my wife doesn't deserve to cop anything publicly. She's the mother of my children. Surely you can understand that?' He said this soothingly but I felt a bite of anger rising in his voice.

I didn't know what to think—Was he telling the truth?—but I knew I couldn't be with him until the court case was over. If the case ended badly, though, what then? I forced myself to decide, and then I made myself speak.

'I can't do this anymore, Hugh. I want to be with you but I can't be with you like this. If I can't have all of you, then what can I have? Please don't call me or text me. I need to learn to live without you again.' As I felt another bout of tears welling up in my eyes I knew that I believed every word I was saying, even if it was killing me. I heard him sigh, then he paused before responding.

'I'm so sorry, Ava. This is all I can give you right now. I don't want to lose you but I don't want to cause you any more pain.' His words ripped my heart apart and the ache inside intensified as he began to kiss my tears away. I wrapped my arms around him ferociously and knew that I had to let him go.

He lay with me until I fell asleep in his arms. I felt him kiss my forehead before he left and I knew that it was goodbye.

When I woke the next morning my heart was heavy. I had no motivation to move, I just wanted to curl up into a ball and never leave the hotel room. The events of the previous night hit me like a freight train. How was I going to live without him? For just a moment I allowed the pain to take everything I had left and consume me. I cried until I couldn't cry anymore, and fell into a deep sleep with the silent prayer that I wouldn't wake again.

#FifteenthConfession

Over the next few weeks my life became so dull I couldn't imagine light ever filling it again. As much as I believed I had made the right decision to leave Hugh, I also felt like I had made the biggest mistake of my life. I toyed with the idea of running to him and telling him exactly that, but I remained strong. I needed to move on if I wanted any chance of maintaining a friendship with him, which was something I had to make happen—I couldn't give him up fully or I would crumble.

I buried myself in my work, doing anything I could get my hands on. I was never short on things to do at work but I found myself seeking out new projects to fill any spare time I had. I knew I might be setting myself on a dangerous path that could see me burning out early on my career, but it seemed preferable to confronting the loneliness I felt without Hugh. I began to seek out new clients with globally renowned names—anyone who could be a challenge or a handful—to make sure I would always be busy. With my growing reputation, these kinds of stars seemed to come easier to me.

We continued to talk over the next few weeks, and although the emptiness was torture for me I knew it was just as hard for him to talk to me without being able to share his feelings. Every time the conversation headed in that direction I would cut him off and abruptly end the call. I wasn't ready to hear his excuses and I didn't want him to lie to me. My heart couldn't take any more and I knew that if he said everything I desperately wanted to hear I would end up exactly where I had been, with no hope of anything ever changing.

After my court stint I had no involvement in Hugh's case; obviously the prosecutors had realised I was telling the truth and had reluctantly returned my phone when they were unable to find any evidence that I was hiding something. As relieved as I was that I was finally able to put it all behind me, I couldn't help but keep track of everything he was going through. I waited with bated breath each time a news alert popped up on my screen, and opened it hoping to god that the words 'Not Guilty' would be written somewhere within the article. With every twist and turn I found myself wanting to console him but it was no longer my place. I had made my choice and I had to be strong enough to stick to it no matter how heavily it sat on my heart.

I couldn't really talk to anyone in my family about my relationship with Hugh. For a long time I kept the relationship and my concerns about it to myself because I didn't want my parents to think any less of Hugh, whom they had met at many work functions. When I first told my mother I was seeing him, she was shocked. She wasn't bothered by the age difference between us, but she was worried about my mixing my personal life with my career.

It was the reaction of my stepfather (whom I call Dad) that surprised my mother and I the most. I thought he might be worried by my involvement with Hugh, but instead it seemed that as long as I was happy, he was happy for me. My mother told my father about Hugh and I when I was at their house one Friday night. To my surprise, he lifted his gaze from his book and spoke only one single sentence.

'I knew that they would end up together from the moment I first saw them together. It was obvious in the way he treated her.' Then he lowered his head and continued reading his book. I was completely thrown by how sure he had been after being in our presence for such a short period of time, when my head was such a mess trying to figure out every detail, no matter how big or small, of my relationship with Hugh.

After weeks of torturing myself and my closest friend with every detail trying to figure out where it had all gone wrong, I got sick of hearing the sound of my own voice repeating the same sentences and finally gave up trying to find an answer.

It was at that moment that one door closed slightly and another opened, letting a little light in and bringing David into my life.

I had read a book he'd written about his career in the entertainment industry and various jail stints. I'd been enthralled by his colourful past and wanted to turn his book into a television series. I contacted him via Facebook, and from there we got to know each other through our messages back and forth. After a few weeks he asked to meet me, and I agreed.

I was a little nervous to meet David. While I knew about his past and everything that he had done I still found him insanely attractive in that bad-boy way. What I didn't expect was that he had a heart of gold and was incredibly romantic. I wasn't looking for anything new, but I was surprised by my instant attraction to him.

I was nervous the day I went to meet him. He had flown into town for a funeral and I agreed to meet him at the airport as he waited for his departing flight. I wasn't sure why I felt the need to meet with David, but I was excited.

As I walked to the terminal I heard the announcement that his flight was not far off boarding, so I hurried to the gate battling the butterflies in my stomach the whole way.

I noticed him in an instant, and as he locked eyes with me and walked confidently towards me I realised just how tall and gorgeous he was.

He quickened his pace before picking me up and swinging me around in an embrace that shot the air out of my lungs.

'Hello,' I said when he finally put me down.

He put his hands on my shoulders and took a step back, shaking his head. 'Wow . . . You look beautiful!'

I felt myself blushing bright red. 'Thank you,' I responded reluctantly, trying to accept his compliment. I think what attracted me the most to David was the fact that he was uncomplicated, he was single, a few years younger than Hugh and seemed so open about his life when Hugh was always so closed off.

We talked for about ten minutes before his flight was called and I began to regret making the meeting so short. As we said our goodbyes I felt very curious about him. The thought of Hugh flashed across my mind for a fleeting moment and it made me smile—maybe this was the distraction I needed. A sudden warmth spread through my heart at the thought that I might just come out of a heartbreaking situation in one piece.

As David walked away towards the gate I admired the confidence that he exuded. I found myself imagining him as the kind of man who would pick me up and throw me down on the bed before ravishing my body with such sexual skill that I would be taken for the ride of my life—and that excited the hell out of me.

I watched his muscular body stop in his tracks and spin around to face me. My heart skipped a beat as he rushed back towards me and before I knew it I was imagining what it would be like to kiss him.

He stopped right in front of me with a furrowed brow, as if he was struggling to find the right words to express whatever it was he was trying to say. I had made up my mind that whatever it was, my answer was yes.

'Can I ask you something? You aren't Hugh's girlfriend, are you?'

In that instant I was hit like a tonne of bricks with reality, and I remembered that he knew Hugh.

'No,' I answered swiftly but honestly.

I was immediately grateful that he had to board the plane; I didn't want David to see behind my mask. I felt my confidence unravel at the mention of Hugh's name and realised that I was in so deep with Hugh that I really wasn't ready for anything new.

After studying my poker face he kissed me on the cheek and left like a gentleman. His broad shoulders tensed as he walked and I found myself in awe of him again. He certainly looked after himself but he had one major downfall . . . he wasn't Hugh.

After our first meeting we talked more and more frequently, and I arranged to fly down to meet with him again a week later to discuss the opportunities I had researched about turning his book into a television series. Although I was attracted to David I still wanted to keep things professional.

The day I was due to fly out Hugh called me; he had found out I was coming to town. I had dreaded the moment because I knew what would come next. When he asked if we could meet for coffee I had no reason to say no. Although we had broken up, I knew we had to be civil. We had a few projects coming up together and I didn't want any residual tension to get in the way. I needed to see him and find out if he was okay, so I agreed reluctantly. I wasn't ready to see him face to face but I knew that I couldn't hide from him forever.

He insisted on picking me up from the airport, and after I checked into my hotel we went for coffee. We made small talk, avoiding the giant elephant in the room, but I still couldn't look at him. I struggled to be in his presence let alone discuss anything remotely personal.

I made an excuse to leave less than an hour later, and it tore my heart in two. He tried to stop me from leaving but the look in my eyes told him to let me go. I wished it wasn't like this between us, but I couldn't change the way I felt.

David and I had agreed to go for a drink that night, and at seven-thirty we met at the bar across from my hotel. I had definitely put a bit of effort into my appearance when getting ready to meet with David, but it was different from last time. I still wanted to make a good impression, but this time I was focused on my job.

When we arrived the bar was quiet, but it soon filled up with football fans shouting at the TV screen, and we weren't able to concentrate on our conversation. As we sat there I realised that we had become friends, and deep down I knew that we were never going to be able to work together, despite how much I believed in his book. It was too close to Hugh.

After an hour and a few glasses of wine I suggested we go back to my suite to watch the game. I didn't want anything to happen between us but we were getting along really well, so I didn't want our time together to end just yet.

When we entered my suite I was suddenly filled with nerves, even though as I sat on the couch and he sat on the bed we merely continued our conversation and watched the match.

Soon my discomfort began to overwhelm me and I started to play with my hands, no longer able to concentrate on the match.

'You don't have to be so far away. Come over here; I won't make a move,' he said, looking at me with innocent eyes.

As I made my way over to the bed and sat beside him I could feel our mutual attraction radiate around us. Midway through our conversation I turned to look at him and before I knew it we were kissing.

It took me by surprise as the heat within my heart rushed through my body with such a force that I felt the lust and desire pumping through my veins, the hunger in our kiss growing until I found myself removing his shirt almost on instinct.

He took charge and rolled me over, positioning his glorious body above me. I ran my nails down the length of his arms and back, gripping his muscles tightly as I had imagined doing many times before. I lifted my body towards his but he forced me to stay in one place. I was excruciatingly attracted to him.

I loosened the buckle on his belt and he finally caved, letting me take control. He placed his hands on my waist and began to lift my shirt. I felt a cold shiver run down my spine as his bare skin made contact with mine and I stopped what I was doing so abruptly that I felt my entire body recoil.

He looked into my eyes, searching for answers, but before he could catch a glimpse of the terror that was suddenly consuming me and before I could let it take over completely I began to kiss him again, wishing away the horrible feeling in my gut. Part of me wanted it to be Hugh beneath me, but I couldn't turn back now.

That moment of hesitation kept repeating on me as I felt the alcohol course through me and allow me to relax a little. This time it was David's turn to hesitate as I undid the button to his jeans and set him free . . . and boy was I surprised.

He was very well endowed, so much so that I felt excitement mixed with apprehension for what was to come.

With one swift motion he placed his hands on my shoulders and lifted me off him before climbing off the bed. It was like a slap in the face; reality caught up with me and I felt like a deer staring at headlights as he began to dress.

'What the fuck?' was all I managed to say as I shook my head in amazement at how quickly everything was happening.

He turned to look at me sitting on the bed, confused and vulnerable.

'I just can't do this to you,' he muttered before grabbing his wallet and walking out of the suite.

It took me a few moments to realise what had just happened before I climbed off the bed and opened the door to find him standing at the elevator. I repeated my last statement before he turned and looked at me.

I felt so embarrassed, rejected and confused. I think the anger that flowed out of me was mainly directed at Hugh and how he had let me down, but I couldn't stop feeling hurt by David's actions, which amplified my fury.

'Screw you, then!' I yelled.

I turned to slam the door but before I could I felt the full force of his hand on the other side as he pushed it open again.

I stepped back and let it swing open to see him standing there speechless. He looked torn up.

'I can't do this to you. I've made such a bad habit of sleeping with women and never speaking to them again, and I don't want to do that to you. I *won't* do that to you . . . There's something special about you, Ava.'

Before I had the chance to respond the doors to the elevator opened and he strode into it, leaving me gobsmacked.

I didn't bother to chase after him. I didn't bother to message him. I just closed the door. I walked back through the suite, picked up my phone and cigarettes and made my way to the rooftop.

I sat on the deck chairs by the pool overlooking the city in silence and darkness. As recent events replayed in my mind, tears ran down my cheeks. I wasn't angry with David, I was furious with Hugh. How had I got myself into such a predicament and allowed myself to be so messed up over a guy?

My life had been a lot less complicated before I knew him, yet I knew that there was no undoing what had happened between us. I was in love and it was about time I started accepting that because it wasn't going away. As I sat and watched the city below me my mind tortured me with the same question over and over: was it too late to get him back?

#SixteenthConfession

#COAMMPlaylist
'Dare You to Move'
Switchfoot

I stayed in contact with David but we both understood that nothing more could happen between us. I appreciated what he had done and the respect he had shown me, but I don't think he ever really believed me that I wasn't with Hugh. David liked us both and realised he didn't want to get involved in something that could end badly for all of us.

It was now Hugh I was focused on, and after much thought I sent him a message saying that I wanted to fly back down and meet with him. He seemed excited, which put a smile on my face. It was comforting to think that he seemed to have missed me as much as I missed him, but so much had happened since we had split that I wasn't sure that I was going to feel the same way when we were face to face. That thought scared me more than I cared to admit—I had invested so much in him already.

A few days later I made the trip, and throughout the flight I fought with myself over whether I would tell him what had happened with David.

As always Hugh was waiting eagerly for me when I landed. I climbed into the car and he kissed my cheek, and then kept hold of my hand the entire way to the apartment I had booked. It was clear he was on his best behaviour and was behaving like the perfect gentleman.

By the time we arrived we had agreed to order in dinner. The ongoing court case was one reason we wanted to avoid going out, but I also wanted to spend time alone with him.

While he parked the car I checked in, and the moment I crossed the threshold my heart ached. I knew what I wanted but despite all my plans I had no idea how to get it with someone so complicated. Nothing had changed with his circumstances and that riddled me with guilt as I contemplated reprising my role as his mistress . . . if that's what I was.

A few minutes later I heard a knock at the door and had to grip the bathroom counter to steady myself to take a deep breath in. There was so much to say, and I had to find exactly the right words.

As I opened the door Hugh stood there for a few seconds, drinking me in before he bolted towards me, placing his hands firmly on either side of my face and forcing me back a few steps as he crushed my lips against his.

I heard the door click behind him but I didn't move an inch. My arms remained by my side. I stood frozen to the spot as he kissed me and tears streamed down my face. He pulled away from me, gently wiping the tears from my cheeks. He placed his head gently in the crook of my neck, pulling me closer to him until I threw my arms around his neck.

'I'm so sorry, Ava,' he whispered ever so softly in my ear.

I gripped him tighter, the tears still falling as I responded. 'Please forgive me.'

I felt him tense. He released me a little and held me at arm's length. 'What do you have to apologise for? It's my fault—I shouldn't have got you mixed up in all of this.'

I turned away from him and reached out to the couch in front of me to steady myself. The knot in my stomach was growing by the minute as I contemplated telling him about my night with David; despite everything Hugh had done, I felt guilty. Hugh was the person who had originally told me about David's book, and he knew that I had made contact with him about turning the book into a series.

He moved behind me. 'Ava?' he said carefully.

I forced myself to sit before I passed out or my legs gave way. He slowly sat next to me, keeping his distance.

'Hugh,' I began. 'I caught up with David Estrich a few weeks ago and . . . I almost slept with him. I would have if he hadn't walked out.' My body trembled and tears filled my eyes but I forced myself to continue. 'The reason I let it go so far was because I was angry with you, and angry about our situation. I think I was mostly pissed because I felt like I couldn't do a single thing about it!'

I saw Hugh's eyes darken as his face turned to stone. He was quiet for a few seconds, gathering his thoughts before responding. 'I understand,' he said through gritted teeth.

'I promise there's nothing there,' I said quickly, 'and I won't be sleeping with him. It was a moment of weakness and vulnerability. I'm so sorry.'

'Ava, this isn't your fault. I'm angry with myself. I drove you to someone else and I can't take that back. I don't want to hurt you,' he said.

My phone began to vibrate on the table and as I looked down I saw David's name flash up. He knew I was in town and had been asking me to catch up all day. Before I could do anything Hugh's eyes flicked to the phone, and he took a deep breath in.

I tried to ignore the phone but Hugh continued to stare at it. Eventually I grabbed it to turn it off but he told me not to. I opened the message in front of him but he couldn't even look at it.

My bones chilled as I read: David's text asked me if I would like to see him for dinner. I turned to Hugh, not knowing how to respond and looking to him for answers.

'Do you want me to drive you to meet him?' he asked.

I was dumbfounded. 'No!' I said sternly.

'Why not?' he snapped.

'Because I'm here with you, and this is exactly where I want to be,' I said angrily.

He studied my face until I couldn't bear it any longer. I closed the gap between us and knocked him on his back on the sofa, pinning his hands down beside him as I kissed him gently. We linked our fingers and I began to feel the ache of desire return.

A knock at the door interrupted us, and as I pulled back Hugh jumped up swiftly to answer the door and collected dinner from the waiting attendant. I sat there, sure I looked a total mess.

As we ate dinner I couldn't ignore the icy feeling between us, but later as I lay in his arms watching a football game I felt warmth again. I realised in that moment as he yelled at the television that this was what I wanted—simply, to be with Hugh.

I left him to the game and moved to the bedroom, where I changed into my white lace underwear and black silk nightgown. I stood in the mirror, fluffed my hair and let it fall nicely around my shoulders. I lit some candles and called out to Hugh, asking him to help me with something.

I stood by the bed as he walked in and stopped dead in his tracks as he saw me. My vulnerability and fear of rejection had me shaking a little inside.

He walked over to me and placed his palm around my chin. I looked into his eyes as I put my hand flat on his chest until he kissed me and lifted me up. He wrapped his arms around my waist while I lifted my legs and encircled his hips. It felt so natural and easy to return his kiss as he laid me down on the bed and hovered over my body. He ran his hands through my hair and briefly stopped kissing me to take in my features.

I wondered if he was having second thoughts, so I began to unbutton his business shirt before sliding it off his shoulders. His intense gaze stayed on me as he loosened my nightgown, never breaking his concentration as he searched my eyes for my inner thoughts.

We made love for three hours. Slowly and passionately, never looking away from each other. I felt every breath, every motion, every tingling sensation that erupted as he ran his hands over my body. In those hours I realised how much I loved the man and knew that I had made the right decision—I was right where I belonged.

As I lay in Hugh's arms, with him kissing my forehead and running his fingers from my shoulder down to my elbow, I knew that he would have to leave soon. I didn't want him to go but it was the way things had to be. I knew I would have to say something, to tell him how I felt but I couldn't do it that night . . . I only knew that if I didn't do it soon it would break me.

#SeventeenthConfession

#COAMMPlaylist
'Think Twice'
Celine Dion

I left Hugh's arms feeling even more confused about where I stood with him. I knew what I was doing and what the possible consequences would be but I didn't care because I had him back in my life.

Whenever I question myself or my choices in life, I run to the one thing that I am sure of, the one thing that makes me feel safe and loved—and in this case, that something was Hugh. He had taught me so many things and given me so much that even after everything we had been through I could never hate him or shut him out of my life.

When it came to the questions I had regarding his marriage, I found it harder than ever to even think about what he did when I wasn't around. I didn't want to know if he was still with his wife or if he was sleeping with her. It might seem difficult to understand, but I found it too painful to even phrase the thoughts in my head. Nevertheless, these thoughts would creep into my head at unexpected moments, contradicting the positive and happy thoughts I'd had only moments earlier. I was never sure whether I was just reading too much into things or subconsciously sabotaging my own happiness, which I had done many times before.

Two weeks after our reunion Hugh went to court. I held my breath as I awaited the verdict of one of the biggest media events to take over the country. It was on every channel, in every newspaper—everywhere I went someone was covering the case. I couldn't escape it. Then came the verdict that shocked the nation: not guilty.

My heart collapsed within itself when I heard the words. Finally, it was over. I couldn't wait to speak to him, congratulate him and hug him—until I realised it still didn't change anything between us . . . did it?

I called Hugh that night, and as soon as I heard his voice I felt at ease and knew that I was going to be okay.

'How are you?' I asked cautiously.

'Fucking pissed off. I haven't had the time to really take it all in, I've been in meetings all afternoon with the lawyers and planning our next move. A lot of heads are going to roll for trying to make me the scapegoat for something much bigger.

It's far from over, and I know exactly where I'm starting . . . at the top!' he spat.

I knew he wasn't angry with me, he was furious at the situation. He knew exactly why this had happened to him and he was planning to stir up a shit storm against the people responsible. Hell hath no fury like Hugh Montgomery!

A week after the verdict was announced one of the people responsible handed in their resignation and all of a sudden the dots started to add up. I didn't know what Hugh was planning but I was very glad I wasn't in the firing line.

He made plans to visit me, and for the first time I found myself wishing that he wouldn't. I really needed to clear my head; I felt so out of control when it came to him and I knew that I would bend again to any of his needs or wants. I wasn't sure if I was ready for whatever the future held, or if I would survive the unknown again.

The day he was set to arrive I still wasn't settled. I found myself getting through the day on autopilot until the time came to meet him at his hotel. He wouldn't arrive until ten that night, and the fact that I was to show up at his hotel that late made me feel like a hired call girl. I had never felt like that before, and I couldn't help but worry that the hotel staff would make the same assumption.

At eight that night I arrived at the hotel to settle into the room he had booked us and get some work done before I saw him—the same hotel in which Hugh had first kissed me.

I couldn't help but smile at the memory as I walked across the marble floors to the reception desk.

The manager was called and I was greeted in the same effusive way as that occasion over twelve months ago.

'Bonjour, Mrs Montgomery. Your suite is ready, and if you need anything please do not hesitate to let me know.' I didn't correct him, I just took the swipe cards and headed to the elevator.

Standing in the empty hotel room I felt a wave of fear wash over me but I didn't understand why. To preoccupy myself I ran a spa, lit some candles and lay in peace for an hour.

When I finally got out I found myself struggling to make simple decisions without second-guessing myself. I felt panic building rapidly and knew I had to calm down if I was going to be sane by the time Hugh arrived. It was irrational but the nagging feeling inside me just wouldn't go away.

I pulled myself together enough to get dressed. I slipped on my satin baby-doll lingerie, piled my brunette curls into a ponytail and walked into the bedroom to close the blinds.

I felt like I had performed this routine so many times that it was becoming a ritual. Before I could let my mind go into overdrive I turned on the television, pulled out my laptop and kept myself busy by answering emails while lying on the bed waiting for him.

Just as calmness began to engulf me, I heard the door to the suite click and I held my breath as Hugh walked into the bedroom. He was dressed in an immaculate business suit and carried his suitcase. The sight of him was utterly captivating.

He stopped in the doorway and looked straight at me. I felt the fire simmering inside me; I couldn't think, I couldn't breathe, I couldn't move. He walked over to me, leaned down over the bed and kissed me softly on the forehead, then on my cheek until finally he knocked the breath from me when our lips connected.

Knocking my laptop aside he threw his arms around my waist and lifted me from the bed and held me. I felt a rush of emotion take over my body and soul as his hands wrapped around me. I inhaled his cologne and closed my eyes as every memory we had made came flooding back into my mind's eye. He knew how to calm me, he knew how to make my heart race or stop but more importantly he knew how to make me feel the safest I had ever felt in my life without uttering a word.

Right at that moment I wasn't hungry, I wasn't tired . . . I was numb. He let go of me after kissing me softly and went to have a shower. I sat in the same spot for a few minutes before packing up my laptop. As I heard the water run I was tempted to join him. The one language I knew how to speak was the language of sex, and something twisted inside me, telling me my inner demons would be silenced if I made the first move. I knew that once I made love to him my fears of him leaving me, my fears of everything between us, would disappear. The problem was I knew deep down it was only a bandaid and wouldn't really fix anything.

Following our reunion I had gone into this arrangement with my eyes wide shut. I knew where we were destined to end up if his circumstances didn't change and I was not the kind of person who could settle for being the other woman or even a friend-with-benefits. The biggest problem I struggled with was that even though I knew all of this I had never felt a love like this in my life and I was nowhere near ready to give it all up and return to how things were before. Regardless of what happened, I would never be the same. The ache in my heart told me that it would take something serious to break his spell on me and make me leave him.

After his shower he came into the room wearing only a towel. I wanted him then and there. I wanted to feel him inside me, to feel the connection we shared. As I looked into his eyes I could see the same uncertainty that resonated within my heart reflected in his eyes.

Without saying a word he walked over to the bed. I began to move over to give him room but he shot me a look that told me not to move. I sat looking blankly at him; his shoulders squared as he kneeled beside the bed. He took my hand in his and I felt a painfully familiar electric current shoot through me, from my hand to my heart. His silence and the look in his eyes had me on edge. Was he about to end it?

He looked down at my hand, and I lifted it gently from his grasp and caressed his right cheek, tracing lines from his ear to the tip of his chin. He pushed his head into my hand, wrapped his arm around me and pulled me towards him.

I raised myself to my knees on the bed, folding my legs beneath me. With my free hand I ran my fingertips through his hair. He pulled me closer by wrapping his left arm tighter around my waist, resting his head in my lap. My hands stilled in their place as he kissed my wrist hesitantly.

I didn't understand what he was doing, but as I sat there staring at him in a haze of confusion I knew at that very moment it was exactly what he needed. I bent down and kissed his forehead. I placed my hands on either side of his face and lifted his head so I could look him in the eye.

'Do you love me?' he whispered.

I struggled to breathe. My heart screamed *yes* but my mouth wouldn't comply.

'I've never been more afraid of losing you,' he continued softly. 'I couldn't cope if you walked out again, so I've put the house on the market. The process is going to take a while but I need you to be patient with me . . . just don't leave me,' he finished with tears in his eyes.

I sat there stunned, every muscle in my body failing me. I didn't know what was happening. I felt trapped, I couldn't move. I loved him more than life itself, I wanted him more than I had ever wanted anyone or anything—and yet I couldn't say a word. My head screamed at me. Wasn't this what I wanted?

I took a deep breath, closed my eyes and surrendered to everything I was afraid of. Relief and panic washed over me as I opened my mouth, unsure of what I was going to say but knowing full well that it would make or break us.

#EighteenthConfession

#COAMMPlaylist

'End of the Road'

Boyz II Men

'Hugh, I couldn't leave you if I tried—and trust me, I *have* tried. It hurts too much. I want to be with you, but you're going to have to be patient with me too. I've never had to do this before, I don't know how to navigate this minefield and I'm going to make mistakes. If this is going to work I need to know you are here with me. Honestly, my heart can't take any more.'

He looked straight through me. His eyes were filled with sorrow; something inside him had broken. I returned his gaze, looking directly into his deep, dark eyes, and I suddenly felt an overwhelming urge to protect him. He was hurting and I didn't know how to stop it. His pain was stemming from me, but I wasn't prepared to lay all my cards on the table and tell him how much I really loved him. I couldn't—if I gave in I would become more vulnerable than I had ever been and I wasn't prepared to let that happen. We had been seeing each other for almost two years and yet I still couldn't trust that it was real.

He took my hands in his and kissed them softly, then exhaled deeply before pulling away. He stood and walked out of the bedroom, leaving me kneeling on the edge of the bed, frozen. I wasn't sure what had just happened, but I felt like I had just been slapped in the face. I was torn—if I told him I loved him, it would cause me more emotional damage than I cared to admit, but if I didn't say it, what was I risking? As I heard the bathroom door click I turned to look to the spot he had left, whispering, 'I love you, Hugh, more than you will ever know,' as a single tear ran down my cheek.

After fifteen minutes of sitting in the same position I climbed off the bed and did the only thing that seemed to make sense: I grabbed my bag and started to pack.

I pulled out my skinny jeans and white blouse. I laid them on the bed and finished packing up my laptop. I knew that I had to make a choice. If I stayed I wouldn't be true to myself, but if I left I would be completely unhappy. I was stuck between the ultimate rock and hard place.

As I reached for my jeans I noticed a folded piece of paper on the floor next to the bed. I picked it up and unfolded it, and saw a note in Hugh's handwriting. It contained a number of different business scribbles, but what stood out was at the bottom of the page, it had been traced over and over again: *Discuss with the lawyers terms of divorce after talking with Ava.*

I almost dropped the note. Part of me wanted to tear it up and walk out because I was so angry and I didn't know why, another part of me wanted to wipe it from my mind and put it back where it was, but the strongest part of me wanted to walk into the bathroom and wrap my arms around him.

I put the note back in its place and stood staring at it for what seemed like hours. Then, I made my decision. No matter how hard, I had to allow myself to be selfish. I began to dress.

Just as I started to put on my jeans Hugh entered the room. He took one look at me and ran straight over, yanking my jeans from my hands.

'Not again, Ava. I'm not letting you leave again. You have to stop running.' He pulled me closer and I felt every muscle in my body fighting his hold on me. I tried with all my might to push him away but it wasn't possible. I couldn't move.

'Hugh, I'm damaged goods. You need someone who can give you everything you need, you deserve better . . . I can't be what you need!' I yelled at him. I was so frustrated from fighting everything inside me that yearned to embrace the man who had caught my heart.

'Ava, *you* are everything I need, *you* are everything I want,' he whispered. 'No one else compares to you. I can wait for a lifetime, for an eternity . . . whatever it takes. I'm here . . . I'm not going anywhere. I promised you I would never push your boundaries, and I will never break that promise—I wish you could trust that.'

I surrendered to his soothing voice and gave up struggling against his hold. Eventually he let go of me, reluctantly. I stood, too afraid to speak.

He walked around the room turning off all the lights, then picked me up and placed me gently in bed and pulled the covers up. He turned the television on and put the remote in my hand. I couldn't move, I couldn't think.

He walked over to the desk and turned on his laptop. As he settled in to his work I looked over at this handsome figure, this man who so obviously cared about me. It was as though I had forsaken one heartbreak for another: I could finally open up physically but now I couldn't open up emotionally.

After what must have been a few hours I woke to feel the weight of him as he got into bed. He lay on his stomach, and within minutes the change in his breathing told me he had fallen asleep. I rolled onto my side to look at him, but he was facing away from me. The distance between us was excruciating, but I didn't know what to do. I ran my fingers along his back and kissed his shoulder before whispering, 'I love you, forever and always . . . with all my heart.'

Just as I started to drift off Hugh grabbed my arm and pulled me over to him. He wrapped his arms around my stomach, kissing my shoulder as I lay on my side. He squeezed me tighter, whispering in my ear. 'I will never hurt you intentionally, please just trust me,' before he fell asleep again.

I don't know if he heard my admission—we have never spoken of it—but I do know I had never felt so safe in my life.

At about one in the morning I woke and couldn't get back to sleep. I rolled over and began to kiss Hugh lightly on the shoulder as I ran my fingers down his chest and stomach. I could feel his body stir next to mine and I knew what was going to happen next. He pulled me closer with his eyes still closed and I felt the familiar burning electricity in his touch.

I began to giggle because I knew what I was doing to him while he was still half-asleep. I kissed him again on his neck—and then all hell broke loose. He opened his eyes, and the intense look of lust took over my soul as his gaze burned into mine. He wanted me as much as I wanted him. With one swift movement he climbed on top of me and began to kiss my neck as his hands explored every inch of my body. His hand moved towards my thigh and I felt my body squirm, my back arching towards him as I yearned for more. He lifted my nightgown above my head and took off my G-string. He started to kiss me from my stomach to my chest and back up to my neck. My flesh was on fire. I was dying for him to enter me.

He lifted me with one hand under my lower back and slid inside me while kissing me passionately. Our breaths quickened in sync and I wrapped my arms around his neck, pulling him closer to me. I felt every inch of him take over my body, mind and soul, and I wasn't afraid.

I cried out in ecstasy as he sped up his pace, sucking my nipples and nibbling my collarbone as my body moved with his, feeling every movement intensely. Something inside me was letting go of everything I was afraid of.

I manoeuvred my way onto his lap and kissed him ferociously, moving slowly but passionately with him. I could feel every part of my body letting him take me without argument. After an hour we climaxed together, drenched in sweat, and collapsed in each other's arms.

I was utterly blissful. I didn't know what consequences lay ahead the next day once I had left him, but at that moment I didn't care. For once I had done exactly what I wanted to and nothing had stopped me.

I fell asleep in his arms again with the feeling of pure satisfaction resonating within my heart.

#NineteenthConfession

#COAMMPlaylist
'Be'
Jessica Simpson

When I woke the next morning tightly wrapped in Hugh's arms I didn't find myself questioning or regretting my decisions from the night before; instead I found myself embracing them. As always, though, that didn't last long. My heart sank the moment I realised that I had to leave.

I buried my head in my pillow and took a deep, stifled breath before turning to look at the sleeping man beside me. He looked so peaceful. He must have felt me looking at him because he slowly opened his eyes and caught my gaze. I found myself looking closer than I had before. For the first time in over a year I saw Hugh for the person he was: just as broken as me. We lay there for what felt like forever, searching each other's souls, and then I rolled over and tucked myself into the all-too-familiar nook between his shoulder and chest. I thought he would wrap his arm around me but instead he pushed me away. I felt the rejection instantly and I rolled over and searched his face for an answer of some kind, something that would give me a clue as to what he was thinking.

He held me at arm's length and looked straight at me, his gaze unfathomable.

'Ava, this back and forth is driving me crazy. I want to get closer to you but every time I try to I feel like you push me away. You know that if my business wasn't based interstate I would move here in a heartbeat, but I can't. So, I want to ask you something,' he said with a tender touch in his voice.

I gulped. As much as I had learned to trust him, there was still a feeling of uncertainty, which had been steadily growing within me. I didn't know what he could expect from me—after all, he *was* married—and I couldn't see a logical future with him unless his circumstances changed. Then I remembered the note I had found the night before. We hadn't spoken about it and I wasn't in any rush to.

He raised himself on his elbow and continued. 'Ava, I want to see more of you, I want to really try this . . . I want you to move interstate and into the city. I want to be closer to you so I can see you whenever I want—whenever *we* want—and so we can give this a real go. It's not like you can't do your work there. I'll set you up, I'll buy you an apartment and I'll make sure that everything you ever need or want will be taken care of. What do you think?'

I felt the flush of warmth on my skin as I tried not to panic. This wasn't the way this was supposed to go. My head began to scream *no, no, no*. I felt hurt and angry that he thought he could buy me, and I wasn't sure I was ready for what he wanted. No matter what was said, at the end of the day there was a piece of paper in place that stated he belonged to someone else.

All of a sudden I realised that I didn't want to change something that I felt was perfect for me in this very moment.

'Ava?' he said again.

I took a deep breath. 'Hugh, that's a wonderful gesture, and if I wasn't the person I am I'm sure I would jump at the idea. I need you to understand that I don't want to be bought and paid for. I'm not that kind of woman. I don't need your money and I don't want it!'

I could see he was blown away by my reaction, but I couldn't lie to myself any more than I was capable of lying to him.

'Hugh, it's not anything you've done. What I'm trying to say is that I'm not ready. Like I said last night, I don't really know how to navigate through this, and I just hope that you can understand where I'm coming from, because I don't know how else to say it.' I could sense his frustration with me as he buried his head into his pillow before taking a deep breath.

'I understand, Ava, but it doesn't mean I have to like it.

I just can't stand being so far away from you anymore. It's really hard to get closer to you when you're so far away.'

While his words resonated within me I knew that it was going to be hard for me to let my guard down and accept the fact that he genuinely did just want to get closer to me, with no ulterior motive.

I leaned over and kissed him. 'All in good time, I promise. I'm just not ready yet, and someday I hope to explain why.' He looked at me, clearly confused, but he didn't push me, just as he had promised.

Once again we made love slowly and passionately, but it was nothing like what we had shared in the early hours. There was something holding me back this time. I couldn't put my finger on it but deep down I knew it was important.

Before I left, he kissed me. As his lips locked with mine I felt the spark return once more, intensifying my already clouded judgement. I breathed in his cologne just to hold on to him a little longer, to remember what it was that I loved about him. I melted into his embrace, making me realise that he was the only solace I had . . . but did I really have him?

The future was so unclear and I wasn't sure where I wanted things to go because the ultimate ending was so far out of reach. I didn't understand why he was still married to her, what she had that I didn't and why he would want to hold on to something if he wasn't truly with her anymore. Little did I know that in a few weeks' time I would find out those very reasons.

#TwentiethConfession

'Lost Without You'

Delta Goodrem

Hugh and I have always had an intense, once-in-a-lifetime connection. The problem was: the closer I got to him the faster I wanted to run. Not because he had done anything wrong but because my head was telling me that there would never be a happily-ever-after for us. I was petrified that I would be left to pick up the pieces of my broken heart, and so my walls always remained half up.

Two weeks after our conversation I flew into town to see Hugh as well as for a business meeting. I checked into an apartment, and after my meeting with a client I was due to meet Hugh at a hotel for drinks with his friends before moving on to dinner.

I hadn't met any of his close friends in the city and I wanted to make a good impression. Of course I had met his friends in my home city, but this felt different. The man we were meeting was one of Hugh's oldest friends, and the night was very important to him.

I arranged a car service to take me to the hotel, arriving fifteen minutes earlier than we had planned. When I met Hugh in the lobby warmth enveloped my heart. I watched him stride confidently across the marble floors towards me in his business suit, his white shirt undone at the top, and the way he smiled made me melt.

He placed his hand on the small of my back and kissed me sweetly on the lips, then led me up the stairs to the bar. I felt so nervous. I was dressed in my body-hugging white cocktail dress, with my black Kardashian Kollection bag dangling from my arm. I couldn't help fidgeting as we walked towards a man and woman sitting at a table by the bar.

When we reached the table Hugh pulled out a chair for me and introduced me to his friend, Paul. The woman sitting next to him was Paul's personal assistant, with whom he had flown into town to attend a major boxing match.

Paul had ordered me a lychee martini—something I had never had before but quickly grew to love—and a waiter placed it in front of me as soon as I sat down. I watched

Hugh and Paul talk for some time—the PA and I struck up a brief conversation before she moved off to make some business calls—and I enjoyed watching the exchange between the two men and seeing how Hugh interacted with those closest to him. Soon Paul turned to me and asked about my work, and we had a laugh to find that we had a lot in common professionally.

As we chatted, Hugh went to the bathroom, leaving me to talk to Paul on my own. He was a lovely man who didn't live far from me. It wasn't long before his assistant returned and he excused himself to go to the bathroom as well. I couldn't help but wonder if they would meet in the bathroom and exchange notes on me.

Paul's assistant was quite dry, making our conversation a bit stilted, and when the men returned ten minutes later it was like a breath of fresh air had entered the conversation and I found myself laughing with them. We had a few more drinks before Paul and his assistant had to head off to a party, which left Hugh and me alone.

We said our farewells and went to dinner in the hotel restaurant, where we shared a wonderful meal. I think Hugh also enjoyed the special treatment I gave him under the table, and as I wound him up I could feel the desire burning from his flesh radiating in my direction as he grabbed my hand and squeezed it.

After three hours of dinner and drinks we decided to call it a night and head back to my apartment. We walked downstairs, both excited at what was to come; neither of us could wait any longer to tear each other's clothes off. As we were about to climb into a cab I heard someone calling out Hugh's name . . . Paul was back.

Reluctantly we agreed to join Paul for another drink, and a few minutes after we sat back at the bar, the men went to the bathroom again. I found it a little odd that they both went to the bathroom together, but what could I really say?

As the night wore on, Paul gave me his card and asked if we could talk when we were both in town about the possibility of doing some work together. I smiled and thanked him, while Hugh shot daggers at me.

As we left I felt that the night had been a huge success. I had made a fantastic impression on his friend and I thought this would make Hugh endlessly happy, but in the cab on the way back to my apartment his demeanour changed completely and I was confused as to why. We sat in silence, the passion and desire we felt earlier dissipating, replaced by an icy chill.

I pulled out my phone and began to text a friend when Hugh spat out his frustration.

'Are you texting your new best friend Paul?!'

I immediately stopped what I was doing and looked at him, confused and a little hurt. He grabbed my wrist and pulled me closer to him with uncharacteristic force.

'Don't get involved with him,' he said with a look that told me he was serious.

I tried to pull my wrist away but he held on tighter. I looked at him pleadingly and then looked down at my wrist as tears began to form in my eyes from the pain.

'I'm sorry, Ava. There are just some things that you don't need to know about,' he said, releasing me from his grip.

'What do you mean?' I replied carefully as I rubbed my wrist.

'It's nothing,' he replied. I didn't want to pry but my curiosity was eating at me.

We both fell silent as my mind went into overdrive. There were so many secrets between us. I didn't know how to even begin to ask him any of the questions that were playing in my mind.

My heart ached a little more than usual that night as I lay in his arms after we made love. I wasn't really there; my thoughts were a million miles away. I loved this man with everything I had, but I was so confused. I wanted to curl into a ball away from him to clear my head. As I battled my unasked questions—What was he hiding from me? Why the need for so many secrets? Didn't he trust me?—every other little concern I had built up began to pop into my head.

I hated keeping secrets from the people who meant the most to me, and to know that he was keeping them from me made me question how much I was willing to be kept in the dark for. I hadn't voiced my concerns, but it became irrelevant: if he didn't want to share this with me then what else was he holding back, and why couldn't he just tell me?

It made me question what it would take to make me walk away if and when I needed to. There was so much I didn't know about him—but I was determined to find out.

#Twenty-firstConfession

'Take My Breath Away'
Jessica Simpson

After that weekend with Hugh, I started to feel like I was losing myself in the relationship. I really didn't know what we were. I have always had the understanding that there are several types of relationships: friends-with-benefits, exclusive relationship, engaged and married. The problem was, I couldn't fit what we had into just one category. We were more than just friends-with-benefits but we weren't quite in the exclusive-relationship category, so where did that leave us?

I found myself constantly thinking about this over the few weeks we were apart. Nothing had really changed with him. He was the same loving person, the warm and gentle soul I had fallen in love with. I was wildly attracted to him and my feelings hadn't dulled but I knew that something wasn't right. I just couldn't put my finger on it.

I sat in the back of a blacked-out town car on the way to see Hugh at his hotel. He was here for business, and I was aching to be with him. I needed to see that he was still the man—the innocent, pure-hearted person—I had fallen in love with in what felt like such a short period of time. I knew deep in my heart that he was the one, and that I would find it excruciating to live without him.

As I arrived at the hotel I couldn't stop my palms from sweating. My feet were glittering in my crystal-encrusted heels, and I placed one strategically on the ground and took the hand of the waiting attendant, who smiled as he greeted me.

'Bonjour, Madame.'

I stepped out of the car in one swift motion, smoothing down my black tights and white silk top before taking the first few steps forward. I slung my handbag over my right arm, adjusted my sunglasses and fluffed my hair, confident that I looked immaculate.

As I began to walk through the glass doors I was greeted by the waiting bell boys and walked across the marble floor, anxious for what the night ahead held for me. I looked up at the beautiful ceiling of one of the most luxurious hotels I had ever been in and saw the golden chandelier sparkling above me.

I took out my phone and made my way with outward confidence towards the reception desk, praying that the manager would not be made aware of my presence at this hotel again. With all of the confusion going on in my head I wasn't sure that I would be able to handle being called Mrs Montgomery again. I sent Hugh a message telling him that I had arrived. Before I could move to sit near the elevators—I wanted to avoid being noticed by the staff and other guests—a message beeped on my phone.

I know, you look incredible, baby. x

I spun around and in an instant I found him at the bar. He began to glide in my direction down three marble steps and I stood drinking him in, too stunned to move.

It wasn't that he was the most attractive man I had ever seen, but the way he moved with an air of confidence—this time in a pair of Calvin Klein jeans and a crisp white business shirt—always left me with my mouth gaping wide open. Not once did he break the gaze he locked with mine. When he reached me, he yanked me towards him with passion in his grip. As I waited with bated breath for him to kiss me I inhaled his cologne and felt myself go weak at the knees. The only support I had was his arm around me. He took my breath away with his kiss, and once again I felt consumed by the desire, the passion and the overwhelming love that I felt for this man. Every concern that I had ever had about him washed away; I loved him with every fibre of my being, and it didn't matter what he did as long as he made me feel this way and I knew he felt the same. Nothing was going to break our bond . . . this was unconditional love.

Up in the suite I unpacked my overnight bag and then we headed back downstairs for dinner. After dessert we retired to the lounge with a few bottles of wine, where we struck up a conversation with a woman sitting on her own. Hugh knew that I sometimes felt jealous but with this woman I felt completely fine. When Hugh went to the bathroom she turned to me.

'You love him . . . the look in your eyes says it all. The way he speaks to you is beautiful—if you have someone who treats you like that . . . never let him go.' I almost fell off my chair. I was blind drunk after three bottles of wine, and this woman could see straightaway what I had been trying to find out myself, yet I still couldn't believe what she had said.

'I don't know what you're talking about,' I said sheepishly.

'Yes you do, it's written all over your face,' she said confidently.

I was worried she was going to say something to Hugh, so I changed the topic quickly before he returned.

Hugh and I finally said goodnight and as we walked to the elevator I found it very hard to move on my own. I had only been that drunk twice in my life. With Hugh it was hard to let my inhibitions go and just relax, so alcohol was something that allowed me to breathe easily.

When we returned to the suite I felt my body craving him. Before the door even clicked shut Hugh pushed me up against the wall, his hands exploring my body and sending a shiver of delight right through me as his lips touched my neck. He began to nibble on my collarbone and I felt myself becoming excited at his touch. He placed his hands around my waist and pushed himself against me. I began to moan, knowing that I needed to feel him inside me, I needed to feel his hands on my naked flesh; I wanted him so much it began to hurt.

He lowered his head into the crook of my neck and whispered: 'Ava . . . I love you. Please tell me you love me too.' I sensed that there was more he needed to say but in my drunken haze I knew it wasn't going to end well. I instantly began to feel the room spin around me as the alcohol took its toll.

I ran to the bathroom and slammed the door shut before vomiting violently. In my drunken haze I heard him banging on the door, begging me to let him in. Finally he managed to open the door, and I felt his cool hands on the back of my neck as he held my hair back. I felt humiliated. I knew that we would need to talk but I really couldn't have him near me at that moment. I knew that I was vomiting mainly because of the alcohol but it was also due to his confession. This was going to be a long night. I had so much to say and I wasn't sure how Hugh was going to handle it. Was he truly ready? More importantly, was I?

#Twenty-secondConfession

#COAMMPlaylist
'Hate That I Love You'
Rihanna feat. Ne-Yo

Despite what people think, my life with Hugh was not always champagne and roses. I put myself through a lot of emotional torture for no other reason than the fact that I loved the man. In the times when I was unsure how much longer I could cope with things as they were I listened to songs that suited my mood at that moment to help me through the pain. It was when my playlist changed to something promising that all of a sudden I felt myself falling again. I found myself realising that it isn't very often you find a love that is all-consuming and someone who makes you feel safe—and that was why I always eventually picked up my phone and responded to his messages

227

or sent one to sort things out, once again throwing myself back into the very situation I desperately wanted to escape.

After being sick that night I still couldn't manage to bring up what I needed to tell him. I appreciated that, despite the fact we both had so much to say to one another, he always seemed to care more about whether I was okay. Whenever I had drunk too much and was sick he always tucked me up in bed and rubbed my forehead with his thumb.

We had made love in the middle of the previous night and it was as perfect as ever but there was something dry in the air between us. He was waiting for a response and I knew that I wouldn't be able to give it to him any time soon. I needed to breathe, walk away, think rationally and then come back and figure it out with him. I wasn't sure how I was going to talk to him or what the reaction would be, but I knew that if I didn't tell him the truth, I was going to end up bursting.

The confusion I felt when I was with Hugh was out of character for me. I have always been assertive and strong willed, but with Hugh I felt that he had helped me to break through so many of my barriers that nothing made sense anymore. I couldn't imagine my life without him, but I couldn't imagine what my life would be like with him, either. I was so confused, because for once in my life I felt like I was in a place that wasn't always happy and wasn't always sad, but it was a safe place in which my heart could mend. I trusted Hugh's word that he would never push me further than I was ready to go, and even that trust was confusing. It had been a long time since I'd trusted in any man, so what was it about *him* that made this situation different?

When I left the next morning I found myself aching inside. I didn't want to leave him again but I wasn't ready for anything more permanent. I didn't know how much longer he would accept my silence but for now he had to.

I had a pretty normal life when we parted ways. I have family and friends whom I love and adore, I have a hectic, rewarding career that keeps me busy—and at times that's exactly what I need.

A week after seeing Hugh, my best friend came over from Europe. Maria was one of the strongest support networks in my life. Even though we had worked together for five years—from different sides of the world—this was the first time we were going to meet face to face. She knew the deepest, darkest secrets in the dustiest corners of my soul and loved me all the same.

The day she landed at the airport I was a mess, still thinking about Hugh and what I was going to do. I really needed to see her; if there was ever anyone who could see my heart and accept me for everything that I am and everything that I will be, it's Maria.

As I arrived at the airport I was so nervous I wanted to cry. I was excited to finally meet her after all these years and yet something in my heart was making me want to cry, and I couldn't figure out what it was.

After standing at the arrivals gate for more than an hour I saw a short, tanned, dark-haired European princess walk out. I screamed and ran over to her and scooped her up in a huge embrace. I burst into tears, partly because of how happy I felt to see her but also because I knew she would eventually leave.

In the car we talked excitedly, and eventually the conversation turned to Hugh.

Maria turned to me. 'Seriously, Ava, how can he still be in the picture? I will never like him; I hate what he's done to you.'

Even though Maria had never met Hugh she knew all my secrets . . . and clearly she hated him so intensely that she wasn't afraid to say it. I knew that at some point in her trip she might meet Hugh, and it made me suddenly wonder if I was going to have to choose between my best friend—the person I classed as my own flesh and blood—and the man I had fallen so madly in love with. Was blood really thicker than water?

•

A week after Maria arrived we were on a plane headed to the party capital of Australia. One of my clients was performing at a massive party for a corporate giant, and I wanted to be there to support them. I was feeling a little nervous, not just because I wanted the event to be perfect but also because this was the first time I had convinced Hugh to attend an event with me—and he would meet Maria.

We arrived at the apartment I had previously stayed in with Hugh and it hit home that Maria was going to meet him. I was so worried that she was going to truly hate him, and I explained to her that I wished that just one person in my life could see why I was so in love with Hugh. She shook her head, and sadness flooded through me because I knew she would never understand.

As the party got going Maria began to drink and have a great time; I had never seen her so at peace and so happy. Almost an hour later Hugh arrived with one of his clients, and I was instantly drawn to him. I introduced him to people who would be of benefit to him professionally, and I could feel his eyes follow me as I worked the room.

Later in the evening as I stood with Hugh I saw Maria sauntering across the room, drunk. She managed to smile as I introduced her to Hugh. He was his usual charming self and I knew it couldn't be long until the ice queen melted. Surely she had to see what I saw in him, even if it wasn't going to be as easy as one single meeting. She walked away moments later while I stayed by Hugh's side. I knew she hated him but I just couldn't leave him. I was frozen.

Thirty minutes later she returned and told me she wanted to leave the party. I offered to go with her but she refused. She walked straight over to Hugh and whispered something in his ear. A look of shock took over his face for an instant before he whispered back to her and she walked off. I didn't know what to make of their exchange but I had a feeling that it wasn't good.

She returned and kissed my cheek before whispering in my ear: 'I get it, Ava, I completely understand now.' With that she left, leaving me standing there with my mouth open.

When the event finished Hugh offered to drive my boss and me home. My boss climbed into the front passenger seat and as I walked around to the other side of the car Hugh pushed me up against the back of it. He ran his hands up and down my stomach before leaning against me and whispering in my ear.

'What are you doing later tonight?' he said seductively.

'Hugh, I can't; I'm with Maria,' I responded breathlessly. I kissed him passionately, knowing that no one could see us at this angle, before reluctantly pulling away and getting into the car. As he drove he kept looking at me in the mirror and winking. I couldn't do anything but shake my head. When we arrived I half ran into the apartment to track down Maria and find out what the hell she meant.

When I walked into the room she looked beat, and still very drunk. Eventually I got to ask her what she meant about Hugh. She turned to me and shook her head.

'Ava, I know exactly what you mean now. I always believe that someone with a strong handshake is honest and if they can look you in the eye they are truthful—it's something my father always taught me. I saw the way he was with you, he held you possessively and when you walked around the room he kept his eyes on you the entire time. He loves you and it's obvious to everyone. When I left I told him that he had better look after you and keep you safe or he would have me to deal with. Ava, I don't know how you will ever date anyone else. You both love each other so much. I get it now, Ava.'

I actually cried. I couldn't believe I was getting my best friend's approval. It meant more to me than anyone else's ever had. But was I ever going to give myself approval?

It wasn't long after that night that she returned home and a part of my heart went with her. Her words continued to resonate within me as I tried to make a decision about what I was going to do. It wasn't easy but I knew I had to give it a go.

#Twenty-thirdConfession

#COAMMPlaylist

'I Hate This Part'

The Pussycat Dolls

One night, not long after Maria left, I met with Hugh. I was finally in a good place—no games, no stress—and we had an amazingly passionate night.

A few days later as I sat in a coffee shop with one of my employees, working on a new client's media strategy, my phone began to buzz. I looked down at my phone but didn't recognise the number.

'Hello, Ava Reilly speaking,' I said.

'Ava. My name is Tanya. I have some information about Hugh Montgomery that I would like to discuss with you. Do you have a few minutes?'

I was immediately unnerved by the unknown voice on the other end of the phone.

'Tanya, one moment, please,' I replied. My heart began to pound as I excused myself from my meeting. I stood up, holding my phone against my chest. My hands were beginning to sweat and shake as I walked across the crowded coffee shop and pushed open the doors to the busy street. As I exited the building the summer sun beamed down on me and I began to heat up under my black business suit. I felt as though the earth was spinning around me. Who was this woman and what did she want?

I replaced the phone to my ear, with the dreaded feeling that this was not a conversation I wanted to have.

'Thank you for holding. How can I help you, Tanya?' I said, trying to remain as composed and professional as possible.

'Ava, I'm a friend of a friend of yours. A few months back I was in a hotel in the city and I saw you and Hugh having drinks together. I'd seen you once before, about a year ago in another hotel when the two of you were having drinks and I heard a little of your conversations. Later as I walked past the elevator I saw the two of you kissing,' she said. My hands would not stop shaking. Where was she going with this? I found myself pacing up and down the path outside the coffee shop. I felt as if I was the only person there at that point; everyone and everything else disappeared. What did this woman want and how was I going to get rid of her?

I took a deep breath before I spoke. 'I'm not sure I know what you're talking about,' I said as calmly as I could without showing fear.

'Ava, I'm not a threat to you. I want to impart some knowledge that I believe any woman should know,' she responded.

I still couldn't believe my ears. I really wanted to get rid of this woman but I didn't want to piss her off. I didn't want to hear anything she had to say but at the same time I couldn't bring myself to hang up on her. All I wanted to do was call Hugh, but for some reason I felt I wasn't going to like what I heard.

'Ava, that first time I saw you I heard him tell you he was separated. When I told our mutual friend, she thought that it could be true. But at a wedding we went to . . . I'm really sorry, Ava, but I saw Hugh and his wife still very much together. They've never split. He lied to you . . . and I think you deserve to know . . . Hello?'

My world broke into a million pieces. Somewhere deep down I knew it was true but that didn't mean I wanted to believe it. My eyes welled with tears. I took another deep breath in to try to compose myself but it made no difference. The tears began to slide down my cheeks as I felt my heart shatter.

I reached on top of my head and pulled down my sunglasses to avert my eyes from passers-by. I needed a moment to gather my thoughts but I didn't even have five seconds. I knew she was on the other end of the line and if I didn't cover up my relationship with Hugh, it would do more damage to the both of us if she ever decided to open her mouth to anyone.

'Ava, I know this is very hard to hear. I don't want to take up too much more of your time, but I have proof. I'm going to send you a photo I have from the wedding of the two of them together, but I would appreciate it if you didn't mention where you got it. I'm looking out for you. What you choose to do with this information is up to you . . . I wish you all the best and please rest assured that I haven't told anyone else about this, and I won't. I just thought you deserved to know. All the best, Ava.' With that she hung up, leaving me speechless.

I felt sick. So many thoughts crossed my mind. I was pissed off at Hugh. I hated him so much for treating me this way. I wanted to kill him. I had only just spent the night with him not long before, and everything had been perfect. I had finally felt at peace with my life and realised how much I really cared for this man. All that kept playing in my head now was *what the fuck am I going to do?*

Breaking into my conflicted thoughts was a text message— it was from my mystery caller. I almost dropped my phone as I opened the message. There it was, all the proof I needed: my deepest fears stared me in the face as I saw the two of them sitting together, his arm draped across the back of her chair as she leaned forward. His legs were crossed with his hand resting on his knee and his fingers intertwined with hers. They were both staring ahead and smiling. My head began to spin as I closed my eyes, the image now burned into my memory. I closed the offending text and messaged Hugh, telling him to call me urgently.

I wiped the tears away from my eyes and walked back inside. I apologised to my employee, but because she was also a friend she knew that something was wrong. I held my composure and at the moment I was about to continue my phone began to ring . . . it was Hugh.

I excused myself and almost ran outside again. I told him everything that happened, and he went off his tree.

'*Fucking hell, Ava!*' he screamed down the phone.

'Hugh, calm down,' I replied; I wanted to talk rationally. 'I just want to know if what she said is true. Are you still with your wife?' I knew full well what the answer would be but I hoped that I wasn't about to have it confirmed.

'*Send me the fucking photo, Ava!*' he yelled again.

'I will, but please just answer my question,' I said. I began to cry as I sent him the text message that had broken my heart into pieces while I was still on the phone to him. It made me question every single thing he had said but it didn't make me question how he made me feel or even how he felt about me. I knew in my heart that he cared for me, and no photo could take that away from me, but his reaction was causing me to seethe. I had no idea why he was getting angry at me. It wasn't like I went searching for this information; it fell into my lap, and for once I was feeling the anger build up and boil over the top.

'Jesus, Ava! Please stop crying. Yes, it's true. I'm sorry. I know you've known the truth for a while. You've been so distant with me over the past couple of months,' he said evenly but defensively.

'You told me you were separated!' I said hotly.

'We were. Look, I don't go around asking who you're sleeping with! You never tell me anything, so how was I supposed to know that you wanted anything more? I never know how you feel, so I assumed you didn't want anything more, even though I've told you numerous times how I felt. I'm not a fucking mind reader!'

At that moment he received the message. After looking at the photo he explained that it was taken at a christening and that he and his wife were the godparents. My heart dropped. Who was I going to believe? A stranger on a phone, or the man I loved?

I decided that I wasn't going to believe either. I was going to take the situation for what it was . . . but then where did that leave me?

'I don't want to hurt you or your family,' I said finally. 'I'm not going to say anything to anyone.'

'I know, Ava. I completely understand. I care about you and I don't want to hurt you. You know everything now, so it's your choice.'

'Hugh, I don't want to lose you. I just don't know what to do,' I responded, fighting back the tears. It would have been the perfect time for me to have asked more about his life, to get the answers I had been so desperately, silently seeking, but I was so afraid of what they would be. I knew that staying with him went against every moral fibre of my being, but it was Hugh . . . the person who had saved me without even knowing it.

'I understand,' he said. I knew he wasn't going to push me to make a decision on the spot.

We hung up and I stood in the middle of a busy pathway while people all around me went on with their day. What was I going to do?

In that instant a song came into my head: 'You've Got the Love' by Florence and The Machine.

This man was a drug to me. How was I going to let him go? Could I walk away?

My heart begged me to stay, and my head . . . well, it agreed. Before I could think about it any further I sent him a text message.

I don't care. I don't want to lose you. I'm going to fly down next week, I need to see you. I care too much about you to lose you, Hugh.

I loved him, that much I was sure of and nothing was going to stand in the way of my heart, but what was I going to do next?

#Twenty-fourthConfession

#COAMMPlaylist
'Walk Away'
Christina Aguilera

Finding out that Hugh was still married was one of the most painful things I have ever been through. It left me with a lot of unanswered questions and a head full of chaos. The hardest thing for me to swallow was the undeniable fact that I was now consenting to be a mistress, and even though there were no more secrets, the distance between us never felt greater. My heart ached knowing that I wasn't the only woman in his life. What hurt the most was that I knew I wasn't competing with someone insignificant . . . I was competing with his wife, the mother of his children, the woman he had pledged to spend the rest of his life with. The question that kept ringing in my head was: am I really prepared to be the other woman?

For nearly two weeks, I cried. Every time I thought of him, every time I received a text message, every time I heard his voice, every time I saw him in the news and every time someone mentioned him, I cried inside . . . but not for the reason you might think. I cried because I knew the answer to the question that echoed in my soul: I loved him so much I was willing to stand by him no matter what, and that scared me more than I cared to admit.

I never stopped communicating with Hugh over this period of time but I did pull back a lot, and he knew it. He constantly messaged me to see how I was and began to make the kind of effort that at times I felt had previously been missing, but had never wanted to actually admit. There was something about the way he was talking to me and treating me that made me scared of accepting my decision to stand by him no matter the cost but it also made me want to run right back to him and fix things.

Almost a month after receiving the call and photo I had business in Hugh's home town and decided to see him. I was flying in late at night and had a meeting with a potential new client before flying out at midday the next day. I wouldn't have more than twenty-four hours with him, and I decided I needed a beauty transformation to make Hugh fall to his knees, but also to try to give me the confidence I needed to speak my mind to him once and for all.

As I looked in the mirror before I left for the airport I saw perfectly plump lips coated with clear gloss, and smoky eyes that complemented by my golden tan. I had dyed my long black locks chocolate brown to change things up and had straightened them to within an inch of their life with an incredible Kim Kardashian–inspired fringe flick. Adding to my look was the perfect outfit: a long-sleeved white cotton shirt with a V-neck, a pair of my signature hip-hugging black tights that made my legs look endless and a pair of Swarovski-encrusted heels.

The whole flight I felt nervous. At the other end my client, who had also become a good friend, would pick me up and once we had finished our business meeting I was then to message Hugh and we would meet at my hotel.

As I arrived at the airport I felt fantastic and confident . . . by the end of the night Hugh wasn't going to know what hit him. I walked through the terminal with my cream trench coat on, my handbag swinging from my left arm and a pair of sunglasses on to hide the fear in my eyes. This was the first step towards my future; there was no turning back now.

Waiting for me outside was my client, Shaun, in his gorgeous BMW convertible. He jumped out and gave me a huge hug. When I got into his car the smell of leather consumed me. I felt my seat heat up instantly as he turned on the seat warmers. The whole trip from the airport into the centre of the city was incredible. I had never really paid

244

attention to the city at night, but tonight it was incredible; it was lit up as if by fireworks. As we drove through it I felt the familiar rush of my favourite type of season. The frozen air of winter swept around me with the top down while inside the car I felt as if beautiful summer sun was kissing my skin.

The city was in full swing and I was about to throw myself into it. We joined thousands of people as we stepped out into a bustling crowd in one of the most notorious hot spots and suburbs in all of Australia. A TV series had been made about the clubs and the notorious figures that controlled them, but I didn't see anything out of the ordinary as we sat down in a fabulous restaurant for amazing pizza, beer and business.

All around us were people who knew Shaun. Every time we began to discuss business someone would come up and hug him or interrupt us, so in the end we gave up. I was supposed to let Hugh know I had finished my business meeting, but . . . it was almost midnight . . . and Shaun asked me if I wanted to have another beer. I guess I was trying to delay facing Hugh, so I told myself that one more couldn't hurt. Well, one more turned into three and midnight turned into 3 a.m. and a very sober me turned into a very tipsy me. By then I knew that I wasn't going to see Hugh, and I was relieved. Hugh messaged me seven times that night and I never responded, I just couldn't.

Shaun and I were both too tipsy to drive, and I couldn't be bothered heading to the hotel, so I went back to his house.

We stayed up watching *Love Actually* in his room, but nothing happened. We had become fast friends but there had never been a connection beyond that. As the film ended I began to regret not seeing Hugh. I was missing him. Tears formed in my eyes but I knew I had to shake off the feelings. I fell asleep next to Shaun in his bed, and woke up hours later, startled by the unfamiliar surroundings. I couldn't stop thinking about Hugh, so sleep was pretty much out of the question. I just kept staring out the window as the whole night flashed past me. I thought about Hugh and how much I missed him, and the next thing I knew the sun was rising and I was witnessing the most incredible sight I had ever seen. I hadn't been up and alert at that hour in a long time, and in that sunrise I knew I loved Hugh more than ever . . . and I was determined to make it work at all costs.

Later that day I finished my next business meeting and had to get on a flight home to be back in time for an important conference call with the team and an overseas client. I still hadn't contacted Hugh, and just before I boarded I sent him a message to apologise. By the time I arrived home and turned on my phone I had received a text message . . . that chilled me.

'Okay, Ava,' was all he had responded.

I felt horrible but I couldn't do anything to change it. So, I left it. A week later he flew into town but I was away, so we missed another opportunity to talk. The next time I flew into town for business he wasn't there, and the time after that we planned to meet but I came down with severe stomach cramps and I called to cancel—something I had never done before. He was unimpressed, and angry.

This was a month of not seeing each other, and I was starting to feel sick about it—but I knew I hadn't been ready to see him. He called me a week later and asked if I would meet with him while he was in town on business. He sounded completely defeated, but I still couldn't do it. My head screamed *yes* but my heart screamed louder. So, I lied and told him I had to fly interstate. My heart told me he knew it wasn't true.

We began to message back and forth and he asked me outright if I was avoiding him. I told him honestly that I hadn't been, but he seemed convinced otherwise. After our messages grew heated I decided I'd had enough. I had to see him, but I wasn't sure if I could handle it.

My heart was crushed as I felt my pain finally consume me. I didn't know what to do. My decision to be his mistress was morally repugnant in my head but I loved him so much I couldn't see my life without him—and I knew I couldn't bear to see him with anyone else. I was broken, but I didn't know how to fix myself.

I managed to get through the rest of the day going through the motions. I tried to convince myself that I really didn't want to see him, but all the while I knew I did. I knew that in the next few days he would leave on an overseas trip, and I desperately needed to feel his arms wrapped around me, his lips on mine, I wanted to feel the electric touch that had been missing in the past few months. I needed to reconnect with him.

That night at home I couldn't stop thinking about the fact that Hugh was in town less than twenty-five minutes from me—and I was too scared to see him. I was hurt, I was pissed off and I was so in love . . . what the fuck was I doing?

I called Hugh and told him I was back from my interstate trip and I wanted to see him. I could feel his relief through the phone, and in turn I was relieved as well.

'Ava, I knew you weren't going out of town, I knew you were avoiding me. But I knew that in your own time . . . just get here. I'm with a few friends, but . . . we have so much to talk about.'

I hung up and raced to get ready. I made sure I looked irresistible: I put on my little black dress that had a slip of skin-coloured material underneath so it looked like I was just wearing black lace; I complemented this with my crystal heels, and I looked better than ever. On the inside I was sick, but it was now or never.

I packed an overnight bag and decided that I would go to him and whatever happened would be on my terms, not his.

When I arrived at the casino I had no idea what life was about to throw at me next. The question was: was I strong enough to take it?

#Twenty-fifthConfession

#COAMMPlaylist
'Everything Has Changed'
Taylor Swift

As more time had passed, I had begun to realise that our relationship was starting to morph into something so destructive for both parties; that we were moving further and further apart. The physical distance was an issue, but what scared me more was how much I didn't know about this man. There had been times when we were together that I questioned things about our relationship, always putting it down to my insecurities in the end, but then he would say or do something that made me realise how much I loved him and in those moments my insecurities would fade away and I knew that I was making the right decision. No matter how much I tried to deny it, I loved Hugh. There was something between us that I couldn't escape and deep in my heart I didn't want to.

Arriving at the casino, I was excited by the prospect of seeing Hugh, but more importantly I was frightened. We had not seen each other since he had confessed that he and his wife were still together, and if I wanted any hope of finding out what this meant, I had to get myself together. One of the things I had learned about Hugh was that if I wanted something I had to come out and say it. If I didn't, then he would shut down. He hated games, and so I had to find the courage to be honest with him.

I walked up the cream stone steps and across the marble floors, hearing the familiar click-click of my heels as they hit the floor. My heart pounded and my head swirled. The closer I drew to him the more my skin began to jump with nerves. I made my way through the club and stood in the doorway to the main floor.

As I surveyed the room I saw dozens of tables and hundreds of patrons laughing, drinking and pissing away money as though it grew on trees. I dialled his number, and when he answered it was as if fate had wanted me to find him.

'Where are you?' he bellowed sweetly yet desperately as the crowds parted in the middle of the aisle and there he stood, scouring the room.

I straightened my dress as he made his way towards me. He was still mesmerising, his dark-brown eyes with their golden glint boring through me in an instant. In one swift motion he dodged a passing couple and strode towards me, still on the phone. He was more relaxed and even more disarming than I remembered. It felt like the first time we had met at the hotel. He finally hung up as he reached me and with one rapid movement he flung his arm around the small of my back and pulled me closer to him. I could feel the desperation pouring out of him as he held me there for a few minutes, crushing my airway as I wrapped my arms around his neck and rested my head on his shoulder, ignoring the nosey onlookers. I breathed in the familiar cologne he wore as the fondest of memories came flooding back and I found myself smiling.

I finally extracted myself from his grip and he grabbed my hand. 'Never let go,' he whispered, looking straight into my eyes as he pulled me in line with him and we walked across the main floor to his friends.

After weaving in and out of the crowded floor full of happy punters, we arrived at a poker table where three people sat concentrating on their hands. Hugh walked up behind one of them and greeted him as Charlie, patting him on the shoulder. The man turned around to face us and Hugh introduced me to Charlie and his wife. Charlie shook my hand while his wife gave me the once-over, obviously sizing me up and not liking what she saw.

I bit my tongue as she gave me a filthy look. I don't know what I had done to piss her off but it was clear that there was something about me that she didn't like. Maybe it was the fact that she sensed something more between Hugh and me, but I couldn't be certain. At that moment she noticed that Hugh was holding my hand and her jaw dropped. I instinctively tried to pry my hand from his grip, but he merely squeezed my hand tighter. I couldn't handle her scrutiny any longer and I just wanted to leave . . . preferably with Hugh, alone.

A few minutes later a man approached the table and Hugh, without releasing my hand, introduced me to Shane.

'Lovely to meet you, Ava. Hugh, she's gorgeous!' Shane announced as he shook my free hand. I couldn't help but blush. As Hugh pulled me towards the exit Shane saw his hand clasped around mine—he smiled and winked.

As we walked down the stairs behind everyone Hugh brought my hand behind me and placed our hands on the small of my back, steadying me as I took each step with tender care, walking as quickly as my heels would allow.

We found a cab and began to pile in, heading back to the hotel. Hugh climbed in first with his back to me and, still holding my hand, began to pull me towards him, but as I began to step in the glaring wife forcefully pushed me aside and jumped into the cab. As I hit the side of the cab my hand slipped and I was forced to let go of Hugh's. Shane caught me before I fell any closer to the ground, steadying me with his hands carefully placed around my hips. As I regained composure and thanked Shane I saw the look on Hugh's face. He was panic stricken, not only for my safety but also because I had let go of his hand and he had no idea why. I had landed in the arms of another, and I smiled as Shane helped me into the cab.

Everyone else was oblivious to what had just transpired. I sat opposite Hugh, waiting for the same warm smile to creep across his face as the rest of the group laughed and talked the entire way back to the hotel. I felt so out of place as I saw Hugh's absent expression. He looked out the window in silence with his elbow perched on the window lining and his chin resting peacefully on the back of hand. He was thinking, but about what I had no idea.

I clutched my bag harder and tried not to let his behaviour get to me. He was blocking everything else out. He knew he was losing me, it was killing him . . . I knew it, I could feel it. I could see the conflict ticking over in his head; he was at a loss as to what to do about us, and he was just as confused as I was.

The wife had achieved what she had wanted. She was trying to separate us and she had just opened up the gulf again. I looked at her and she narrowed her eyes at me. She had been watching me the entire drive back and before I turned my head away I saw a sadistic smirk cross her face.

As we arrived I placed my hand on Hugh's knee and smiled at him. He flinched at my touch before he looked me dead in the eyes. I knew that look: he was in another place, so far away from me and yet so close. I felt the prickle of tears growing in my eyes, but just as I was about to get out of the cab and run Hugh grabbed my hand and squeezed it, rubbing his thumb across my knuckles.

The wife witnessed this exchange and I saw fury building up behind her eyes as her face grew red.

We all walked into the hotel, but this time I was walking alone while Hugh was up ahead of me with the others. Every time Hugh and I had been in this hotel before we had created incredible memories, the good and the bad had melted together and still made me smile . . . but this time I felt horribly out of place. I needed to get away.

I turned to leave and ran into a tall, dark and handsome man. I headbutted his chin and ran into his body at full force. He placed his hands on my shoulders to steady me before apologising.

'Are you okay?' he asked as I extracted myself from his grip, still swaying from the knock to the head.

'Fine, thanks. Sorry, I have to go,' I responded before attempting to move around him.

'What's the rush? Stay for a drink,' he said with genuine concern.

I looked up and saw his dark eyes for the first time since the encounter: they were warm and inviting, and they held a smile. His hands felt like ice on my skin but his voice was soothing, and he looked at me with such warmth that I found myself mesmerised.

As I stared at this man, unable to speak, I sensed something familiar about him. I was sure I had seen him before but I couldn't quite put my finger on where. I wanted to escape but my curiosity got the better of me.

He watched me, waiting for a response with a smile plastered across his face.

'I'm okay, thank you,' I finally said. 'I really can't stay, but I have to ask, do I know y—'

Before I had the chance to finish I heard a familiar voice behind me.

'There you are!' Hugh called out across the foyer, making his way towards us.

We both turned to look at Hugh as he reached us. Hugh placed his hand on my back and shook hands with the guy I had run into.

'Nicky, man! Where have you been? . . . Wait, do you two know each other?' Hugh said with a perplexed look on his face.

'No, actually we haven't had the pleasure until now. We just ran into each other, literally,' he replied, looking at me.

Hugh looked at me too and I smiled. 'I actually headbutted him,' I said.

Nicky grinned and in that moment I realised who he was—one of the best-known people in our industry, who was constantly being reported on for his personal and business affairs.

'Well, come and join us; everyone's at the bar having drinks.' We walked through the foyer and into the bar. When we reached the rest of the group I sat on the lounge next to Hugh, all the while feeling Charlie's wife's eyes burning into me from across the coffee table where she sat with her husband.

When the drinks arrived I sipped my white wine with care because I didn't want to get drunk in front of these people. They were obviously well on the way but I wanted to stay in control.

As conversation broke out around the table Nicky watched me intensely before opening his mouth to speak. 'So, what do you do, Ava?' he asked, smiling again. Suddenly the entire table went silent and they all stared at me. Talk about putting a girl on the spot.

Calmly and confidently, I responded: 'PR, actually. I work in the entertainment industry.'

'Ava and I have done a lot of work together,' Hugh said, beaming at me. I could sense something building up, and I couldn't help but feel that Hugh was oblivious to it all. These people were his long-time friends and they all seemed to be sizing me up . . . except for Nicky. From what I knew, he was one of Hugh's oldest and most trusted friends.

Nicky kept trying to include me in conversations—obviously he could tell that the wife was freezing me out—but I just wanted to disappear. We discussed who my clients were, and Nicky and Shane were engrossed as I rattled off names.

When Hugh got up to go to the bathroom and was safely out of earshot, the wife addressed me.

'So, Ava, are you and Hugh fucking?' She spoke blatantly.

I was speechless. This was exactly what I had been hoping to avoid. I knew she had it in for me, and I had no idea how to answer her question.

Nicky looked at me, and as much as he looked sorry for me I saw a flicker of curiosity in his eyes. Now I truly felt ganged up on. I didn't know the wife but it was clear she had an angle, so I decided on the safest route.

'We're friends, we have been for ages. I've worked with him for the past few years,' I explained carefully.

'Oh, give it up, Ava. Don't bullshit us. It's so obvious that you're screwing each other,' she spat. Everyone was on the edge of their chair waiting for me to respond, except Nicky, who appeared to have lost interest in the conversation and pointedly looked away.

I glanced around, unsure of what to say or do, praying that Hugh would return.

'No, really, we're friends,' I repeated, sipping my wine and searching for the nearest exit. Before the wife could continue Hugh returned and Nicky announced he was going up to his room. Everything was in slow motion. I needed to get away but I didn't know how to explain it to Hugh. He would be crushed if I left, the wife would have won and I still wouldn't have any answers.

Nicky left and a few minutes later I excused myself. As I headed towards the bathroom I felt someone behind me and realised it was Nicky. I had seen him at the elevators, but suddenly he was outside the bathrooms.

'Ava, are you really not seeing Hugh?' he said as he approached the door to the men's room.

'We're just friends, Nicky,' I said warily.

'I'm sorry to ask after what you just had to handle, but . . . I'm about to head up and have a nightcap. Would you join me?' he said, taking a step closer to me and placing his hand on the small of my back.

'I'm actually going to head home, but next time for sure,' I replied. In a moment of weakness I had hesitated, contemplating taking him up on his offer, but I knew where my heart was and it wasn't with this gorgeous celebrity.

'Not even one drink?' he said, smiling. I can't say that I wasn't tempted, but I wasn't in a clear head space. And I really did love Hugh.

'Sorry. I have an early meeting, but next time you're in town let's catch up,' I suggested before stepping away.

'Have a good night, Ava. It was lovely to meet you,' he said before kissing me lightly on the cheek.

I turned around and entered the bathroom, where I placed my bag on the counter and stared at my reflection. As I washed my hands I reviewed the night's events so far . . . and then it hit me.

I remembered the news reports: Nicky was married with kids. I don't know if I have something tattooed on my head that attracts married men, but in addition to my feelings for Hugh, I definitely didn't have the energy to deal with another one.

The rest of the night was something that I will never forget, as things went from bad to worse in a matter of hours.

#Twenty-sixthConfession

'Stay With Me'

Arlene Zelina

Within an hour of Nicky leaving I could tell that Hugh wanted to be alone with me. His answers became short, and even though he was polite I could tell he was growing irritated that it was getting late and he and I still hadn't talked. It was clear he had also noticed that the night's events (little did he know which ones) were testing my patience and that I was getting quieter and quieter as time passed.

He began to text me, begging me not to leave. We had become adept at hiding our texts around others. He would message me, I would let my phone go for a few minutes, then I would check it and respond before he repeated the pattern.

I said I wouldn't go, but after another hour had passed I was exhausted and Hugh's friends hadn't shown signs of leaving any time soon.

Finally at 2 a.m. I stood and said goodnight to the couple and to Hugh before I walked out into the main foyer. On my way out I texted Hugh to let him know I would wait around the corner and he should text me when they had gone.

As I walked outside and around the corner for a cigarette I felt emotionally and physically drained. I kept checking my phone but there was nothing from Hugh. When I finished my cigarette I headed back into the hotel towards the main desk to ask for a cab. I knew that Hugh would see me, because reception was in the direct line of sight from the bar. Sure enough, as I entered the foyer I heard his familiar footsteps cascading down the stairs as he ran towards me.

'Ava, please don't go. Come up to the suite. We're all going for drinks, it won't be much longer, I promise. I haven't seen them in a long time. Please,' he begged.

I looked at him with heavy eyes. I agreed and limply walked with him into the elevator. As we all entered Hugh's suite I felt a chill rush through me. I had never felt fear in his company, but this situation made me very uneasy. I think it was because I had never arrived at a hotel with him and his friends before going up to a room. Maybe it was my fear of intimate settings, but this just felt weird. I knew that Hugh would never hurt me, but I didn't know whether I could trust these people. I had no idea why I felt this way, but I trusted that Hugh would never let anything happen to me.

I put my bag down and grabbed my phone before sitting on the sofa. The wife sat at the office table and, as the men were occupied on the other side of the room, she began to ask me how I had met Hugh and how long we had known each other. I answered with no elaboration.

'Well,' she replied, '*I* have known Hugh since he was fifteen. He's a real catch, but too many women try to take advantage of him. Don't you dare be one of those gold-digging whores,' she said venomously.

I was gobsmacked. Did I really give off those vibes? I tried to tell myself she might just be trying to protect a friend. The way she spoke to me was wrong, but somehow I understood. I didn't feel it was appropriate for me to say anything to her, because I knew that she would snap. I was already reaching the end of my tether and, being so tired, I couldn't be sure that I wouldn't end up biting her head off.

After about twenty minutes she went to the bathroom and returned jovial. Shortly after, Hugh got up to go to the bathroom. I'd had enough and just needed to be with him alone, at least for a few minutes, so I followed him. As I entered I saw him standing by the basin washing up. He was bent over the bench as I walked into the bathroom and closed the door over. He looked at me in the mirror with wide eyes and a pained look on his face.

A million questions ran through my head but none were able to escape my mouth as I walked towards him. I felt the prickle of tears sting the back of my eyes as he grabbed my chin with a tender and delicate grasp before kissing me lightly. I was frozen. My fear of the situation outside dissipated as my fear for us grew. We still hadn't spoken about his marriage and I wasn't sure if I did open my mouth that anything coherent would come out.

He saw the concern growing in my eyes and he pulled me against his body. He kissed my forehead and held me there for what felt like forever. I breathed in his scent and tried to push the image of what I had just seen out of my head as I closed my eyes. I fought hard to remember why I had fallen for this man, telling myself that he was no different because of his circumstances, everyone has their skeletons and I really wasn't one to judge.

'Baby, please stay. Don't go anywhere. They will leave soon and I really want the chance to talk . . . about everything.' He looked straight into my eyes and I could see the sincerity in his.

Despite all the questions fighting to find a voice, I knew I would struggle to ask him anything. I needed him to come clean to me because I was too afraid of losing him. I knew better than to try to understand what was going on in his head; I had never been married so I didn't know what happened when one person isn't happy and begins looking elsewhere.

What I did know was that no matter what, the strength of my unconditional love for this man was far greater than his circumstances.

•

At 4.30 a.m. they finally decided it was time to leave. I had maintained my silence for the duration of the night, trying my hardest to not show my annoyance, but I was exhausted and I knew I wouldn't get much sleep before I had to wake up again.

As they said goodnight the wife realised I wasn't leaving, and she gave me a look of utter disgust. I assumed she knew Hugh's wife and the status of their relationship, yet I really couldn't care. She hadn't scared me off this time, and in her mind it must have looked like I had won. To me this was not a game; this was my life and my heart. I was gambling with everything I had and I still didn't know where it had left me.

As the door closed behind them I walked over to my bag and pulled out my phone charger, to keep myself busy. I really didn't know how to do this with him anymore. I knew the motions, I knew where it would end up but I didn't know where *I* was going to be when everything was said and done. I felt a little out of place. I still couldn't look at him.

He leaned against the wall in the bedroom with his legs crossed and his arms folded, watching me as I walked around the room. He knew I wasn't going to look at him or say anything. I was too tired to fight; I was too exhausted to think, much less try to sift through the words that had to be said to find what I wanted.

As I took off my white heels and placed them next to the bed I made the mistake of looking up at him. I could feel the vulnerability within me growing and I knew that this man had my heart no matter what, so what was the point of fighting it any longer? I knew that the dance I was entangled in was dangerous but I also knew that my life would be foreign to me without it. It was exhilarating and terrifying.

I moved to walk past him to the bathroom, but at the last moment he stepped in front of me, blocking my way. Still no words had been spoken, but as he placed his hands on my shoulders an electric spark shot up my neck and down my spine, landing in my toes.

He crushed my body against his and his hand moved around to the nape of my neck as he winded me with his passionate kiss. I was instantly knocked back against the wall and felt the burning desire building in the pit of my stomach. I couldn't breathe, I couldn't move and I couldn't stop shaking inside and out. As his kiss consumed me, everything around us faded into darkness. I felt the sting of the familiar violent currents passing through his lips to mine and relished each painful volt as they resonated within my body from his kiss and his fingers that twirled my hair at the back of my neck.

In that moment the currents penetrated the walls I had built around my heart, bringing me to silent tears. I felt the pain, anger and vulnerability escape me and it was then that I knew I was a goner. I was his, and he knew it.

I had felt the desperation oozing from him all night, in his tone, his body language and of course his eyes as he begged me not to leave. Each time I remembered the moments, the tears burned harder and faster down my cheeks. I could not hate this man for putting me in this position because we were both so helpless: he wanted to spare me the pain but couldn't bear to let me go; I was desperate to leave him and give myself a fighting chance at a love that could give me everything I had ever wanted, but I knew that a love like this only came along once. I was terrified of losing it, of never feeling it again, and my heart was breaking because I knew that I could never be the one to leave—he would have to tell me he didn't care, he would have to stop craving me as much as I craved him for me to be able to truly stop. He was the only drug I ever needed and I was undeniably addicted. He was the one.

#Twenty-seventhConfession

#COAMMPlaylist
'Let Her Cry'
Hootie & the Blowfish

When neither of us could breathe any longer his lips left mine and a ragged breath followed as he slid his hand up from the back of my neck and gently rubbed his thumb across my cheek, cupping my jaw with the palm of his hand before resting his forehead on my chin. I was still pinned against the wall, but we both knew that no matter how much we wanted to take things further, it just wasn't the answer.

We were exhausted but we needed to face whatever was coming head on. I gently kissed his forehead before throwing my head back against the wall, closing my eyes and exhaling.

It was the only thing I could do to fight back the tears that were slowly, silently creeping their way down my face.

How had we managed to get to this place where simplicity seemed so out of reach? The longer we ignored our issues the more prominent they became and the more distance they put between us.

I was fighting the urge to pull him close and tell him that everything was okay, that nothing was wrong and just pretend, but I was too tired. Conflicting emotions were building up inside me. The biggest problem I faced was that I really didn't want to lose this amazing man but I knew if I didn't say something I would end up losing myself. Weighing up those options, I knew what I had to do.

I placed my hand on Hugh's chest and gently pushed him away from me. For a moment I thought he was going to get that look in his eyes that meant I had no hope of opening up any form of discussion, but something shifted in him. He seemed calm, scared—and sad. I looked into his beautiful brown eyes and saw a flicker of vulnerability. I took a deep breath in and steadied myself against the wall, trying to keep my balance in my tired haze. We both knew what was coming as the silence grew to a deafening roar and yet neither one of us wanted to be the one to speak first . . . neither one of us wanted to be the instigator of what would surely be our most heated fight ever.

It was like preparing for battle with everything you need to shoot but freezing when it was time to pull the trigger.

Hugh had hung his head. I opened my mouth to speak, afraid that the words in my head wouldn't form verbally, but he placed his hand out to stop me.

'Ava, I know what you're going to say and I'm not going to try to stop you. I won't deny what I have put you through and I won't lie or try to undermine your feelings, but before I face everything, I need you to listen to me. I need you to look deep inside yourself and think about every single thing that we've been through—the good, bad: all of it. I need us both to cut the bullshit, and I need you to give me an honest answer so we can figure out what the future holds. Ava, I need to know: do you love me enough to forgive the mistakes I've made and will make in the future?

'For not having the guts to tell you the truth about my life, and for being so scared of losing you that I've let us both ignore the distance that's been growing as we both hold so many things back? Do you love me enough to wait while I sort out the mess I've made of my life?'

He took a quick breath and continued, as if afraid that if he didn't speak now he would never find the courage again. 'And lastly . . . I need to find a way to make this work, and I need to know—right here, right now, in your heart of hearts—what *is* it that you want from me? For us? Whatever it is, I'll do it. I'll earn your trust, and I'll never hurt you again. I can't promise you that I won't make mistakes, but I *will* work every single day to be a better person than I have been to you, because I simply wouldn't survive if I lost you. You are exactly what I've been searching for as long as I can remember, and now that I've found you, I'm not giving you up without a fight. I love you, Ava. I want you in my life forever.'

He finished so calmly I was completely unnerved. I'd never seen Hugh this desperate, this broken, pleading for my forgiveness. As I stood listening to the words he spoke with such care and soothingly honest tones, I saw the tears welling up in his eyes. I was too stunned to speak, to breathe or even to move. All I wanted to do was slide down the wall and hide my face and thoughts from the world, but there was no possibility of running from everything without breaking his heart as well as my own.

As I contemplated his words with a heavy heart I realised that something inside me had broken beyond repair. I trusted Hugh with my body but I had never truly been able to give him my heart. As much as I loved him, there was something that always held me back. I couldn't blame him solely for where we had ended up; I had hidden my feelings well until this point and I was just as much at fault as he was. It would have been so easy for me to grab my bag and run from the room, never speaking to him again and erasing every memory of our time together, but my feet were planted so deeply in that spot that the thought of moving in any direction felt alien to me. I knew I loved him, but two questions replayed in my head like an echo that refused to end: was it enough and did I have the strength to withstand the unknown?

Within five seconds I knew the answer to my own questions but I couldn't allow the words to come out. I knew I didn't have the strength to fight the unknown—but I couldn't leave Hugh either. Something inside me told me that if I did, I would crumble and wouldn't ever be able to get back up.

I knew that this was a momentous point in my life, and that no matter what decision I made, I would have to live with it.

Here was a man I loved, offering me his heart. With Hugh I knew that nothing could hurt me but him, and that was more comforting than the unknown . . . at least I knew what I was getting myself into. I took a deep breath and struggled to fight back the tears that were so desperate to be released before opening my mouth to speak.

'Hugh, I know that you really want an answer, but I can't give you one that would be honest. I don't know what I want from us, I don't know where this is going to go and I'm too scared to sit here and try to analyse it. So much has happened between us, and the future is something I fear more than life itself. I feel like I'm drowning at the moment because I really don't know which road to take. I'm afraid to tell you everything, because I haven't even got all of this right in my head. What I *can* guarantee you is that I never want this to end. I need to recover from everything we've been through, but I couldn't handle not having you in my life. I'm sorry, Hugh, but that's all I can say right now, because I don't want to make the wrong decision and regret it in the future . . . All I want is you!'

As the tears cascaded down my cheeks I knew I was being as honest as I possibly could but that my life would never be the same. I had closed off a part of my heart to this man, and it would never open again.

I searched his face for answers but found nothing. He took a step closer to me and I had to fight every urge in me to run. I was feeling so vulnerable and lonely as memories of everything bad between us flooded into focus.

But then I remembered all the times Hugh had saved me. I remembered the first time I had let him into my heart, the first time I felt the spark between us and the first time I let him show me his worth.

I still wasn't ready to walk away from Hugh. I loved him more than I could say and in order for me to walk away something drastic would have to happen.

The silence that filled the air was becoming unbearable, and before I could move his hand flew up towards my face and he pulled me in for a passionate kiss that took my breath away. I felt the wave of relief wash over me as I realised that I wasn't going to have to talk anymore.

I felt his free hand travel up my thigh and the familiar burning desire returned as the volts of electricity passed through me from his touch.

I kissed his neck and felt his breath on mine as he lifted me up and carried me towards the bed. I threw my arms around his neck and nuzzled into the crevice between his neck and shoulder. I felt safe, I felt at home and able to keep the inevitable fight at bay . . . for a little while, at least. He placed me gently down on the covers and began to explore my body with such care that the smouldering desire quickly turned into a roaring fire as he expertly found every sensitive spot on my body. He knew it so well; he was still the only person who knew how to make me let go and revel in the moment.

As time passed, I drank it all in. How could I deny myself the love I so clearly felt when I was with him? How could I be so scared when he clearly felt it too? What was I really looking for? Did I really believe that I was going to find something more elsewhere? And, importantly, was I willing to risk all of this for a greener grass I wasn't even sure existed?

In the very early hours of the morning as we lay in bed I thought about whether to tell Hugh about what had happened with Nicky. I was trying to move forward on an honest note and felt I owed him that. Because Hugh and Nicky were so close I tried to put a funny spin on it.

'You know, something funny happened tonight. I could have ended up somewhere else,' I said, laughing.

'Oh really, what happened?' he said, raising an eyebrow with a cheeky grin. Here was the playful Hugh I knew and loved. I was sure he was going to laugh.

'Well, Nicky asked me to come up to his room,' I said, returning his smile.

He sat up straight and a dark look came over his face. This was not what I was expecting and I immediately wanted to eat my words.

'Don't! Ava, that's not funny. I can't *believe* he would do something that fucking stupid. Tell me exactly what happened.' In that instant I knew I shouldn't have said anything. I could feel the rage and jealousy enter his voice as the room turned cold. I sat up and pulled the sheets tighter around me.

'Well?' he demanded.

When I finished the story he grabbed my shoulders firmly before kissing me like he had something to prove. As he released me I let it all go and walked into the bathroom before locking the door and standing against the bench, struggling to gain my breath and desperate to gather my thoughts.

I didn't sleep much during what was left of that night. I was so confused. I needed space, which was impossible when we were sharing a bed. When I finally drifted off to sleep the sun was creeping in through the closed curtains, and a tear fell down my cheek before the world faded to darkness.

#Twenty-eighthConfession

#COAMMPlaylist
'Burn'
Mia Rose

A night of broken sleep never agrees with me. Lying on the opposite side of the bed to Hugh, through the night I had attempted to put as much distance between us as I could. Just as I finally drifted off to sleep I felt my arm being yanked and my body was limply dragged towards him. In my semi-unconscious state I found it almost irritating. He had no idea what I had been tormenting myself with all night as he slept soundlessly beside me, and here I was again being woken up at the most inconvenient time.

I allowed him to pull me close to him and wrap his arms around my naked body, but I attempted to remain limp and I didn't dare to open my eyes. I knew that if I did—if

I showed any sign of being awake—that I would have to face the morning with a smile and push the ever-growing concerns from my mind. I could no longer ignore the feeling that something was off between us. I knew that he loved me, but I could also feel myself resenting him for the pressure he was putting on me without even realising it.

As I lay silently in bed with Hugh's arms wrapped tightly and protectively around my waist, I could feel his breath in my ear as he whispered to me.

'I meant what I said, I *will* prove myself to you, Ava. Just give me the chance.' As he spoke these words I found myself shuddering from the inside out. I felt my heart race and didn't risk moving.

I couldn't help but think of the irony: when he wasn't sharing anything I was petrified of losing what we had and basically threw myself at him, but then there were times when he gave me as much as he was able to and I couldn't run fast or far enough away.

I swallowed hard and squeezed my eyes shut tighter in the hope of blinking back the impending tears that were threatening to give away my deepest feelings and fears. I was more confused than ever about our situation, and all I wanted was to escape into a dark hole as his words reverberated in my head. I felt as though I was losing myself in the transition from girl to woman, and not just any woman: the type of woman I had vowed never to become—a mistress.

As the realisation of my choice set in I felt my stomach stir, I felt bile rise but my throat was too dry and swallowing only made it worse. I lurched forward, sat bolt upright, threw the covers (and Hugh's arms) off me and jumped out of bed before bolting to the bathroom, slamming the door and locking it. I tried to catch my breath, steadying myself against the marble bench, but it made me feel worse, and before I could stop myself I was leaning over the toilet retching. Hugh's whispered words replayed in my mind and each time my stomach lurched a wave of nausea flooded my body. I felt myself burning up as the sweat began to gather on my neck and forehead. Hot tears burned down my cheeks as the memories began to flood in.

As I closed my eyes I saw the women from his past we had run into, I saw the intensity and passion floating between us whenever we were in sync, I felt the split-second panic every time he touched me, I felt the yoyo of emotional torture as the distance grew and retracted between us on a regular basis, and then finally I saw the image that pushed me over the edge: Hayley, Hugh's wife. Her face crept into my head and before I knew it my sight began to spin out of control, my mind and soul felt as though they were splitting in two and I couldn't stop the images and feelings from breaking through my barriers, making me feel like I was in a never-ending merry-go-round, until I felt the dull blow to my head as I hit the marble floor and curled into a ball, silently crying and biting my fist to stop the screams from escaping my mouth.

My conscience had kicked in again . . . I could no longer ignore the one person who would forever stand in the way of my happiness, my future, my hopes and dreams.

Hayley's image was imprinted on my memory and no matter what I did I couldn't get rid of her. I felt so confused, conflicted and unsure of which direction to take. No matter what the choice was I would find myself in a place I wasn't ready to handle, but this place I was in right now was my own version of hell—my guilt was eating me alive and I had no idea what to do. I was so lost, I truly wasn't sure if I would ever get up from the cold hard floor that seemed to be the only thing holding me together but I still feared that at any moment it would open up and the world would swallow me whole.

I had been so numb to the reality surrounding me, confusion poisoning my very existence, and consumed by my guilt and love for Hugh that I hadn't even heard him pounding on the bathroom door, yelling out my name, until after he had broken the lock on the door and burst into the bathroom. He swooped down and collected me in his arms, and his eyes filled with tears as the panic set in that something was seriously wrong. He yanked my white silk robe down from the back of the door and put it on me, gently lifting my limp body as he placed each of my arms in the sleeves and tied it gently around my waist. I felt like an outsider looking down on this situation. I could see it so plainly from above but I was trapped inside my love for him and I just couldn't see a clear

Confessions *of a* Millionaire's Mistress

path. He dragged me back into his arms as he repositioned himself sitting on the floor. I continued to stare at the wall tiles, not registering anything that was happening around or to me. My walls had gone up and nothing but focusing on the safety of that barrier mattered. Behind the wall I was safe. No one was getting in . . . not even Hugh.

'Ava, I don't understand what's going on, but please tell me what to do. I knew something was off last night. It's not like you to go down without a fight. I feel like I'm losing you and I have no idea what to do. I'm so fucking scared. Please, Ava, tell me what to do . . . I can't lose you!'

I heard every word, I felt every quiver in his voice, and as much as I was desperate to fix this situation I couldn't muster the strength. I could feel the exhaustion taking over. I let my head loll back and moments later my eyes followed until I met his and I saw just how genuinely broken he was inside. Just before I drifted off I gathered the last pieces of energy I had left to fight for what I wanted most and let the last tear roll down my cheek as I whispered almost inaudibly, breathlessly speaking the only words I had left, for the very first time while he was awake, before giving in to the exhaustion and falling asleep . . .

'I love you, Hugh.'

#Twenty-ninthConfession

#COAMMPlaylist
'How Long Will I Love You'
Ellie Goulding

When I woke up a few hours later I found myself even more exhausted than I imagined possible. I felt as though I had woken from a horrible nightmare and was terrified of facing the situation with Hugh. I wasn't sure what I would be waking up to, which only fuelled my fears. I was wrapped in his arms in the warmth and safety of the bed, and I could tell by his heavy breathing that he was fast asleep. My mind kept replaying the sequence of events that had played out earlier that morning; everything was still a little fuzzy, making it all feel surreal. I wasn't ready to move but I felt a level of calmness in the air that made it easier for me to breathe. I had told him I loved him but I couldn't recall if he had heard me, and until I had the courage to say it while we were both conscious I wasn't planning on bringing it up again.

After a few moments of peace I felt the need to get up and stretch my legs, which felt numb and constricted by the bed sheets. I knew it probably wasn't a good idea to move but I also knew that I needed a little head space. I was afraid of releasing from the safety of Hugh's arms, but the time had come to try to stand on my own two feet. I slowly began to move, trying not to wake him but failing miserably.

'Ava,' he whispered so softly it made me still, sending shivers down my spine.

'I'm okay. I just really need a shower,' I responded, feeling the quiver in my voice take over.

'Please don't do this,' he said tightening his grip on me.

'I just need a few minutes,' I replied, still facing away from him so my eyes didn't give me away.

He didn't push it any further. His eyes seared into the back of me as I carefully sat up and placed my feet on the floor, praying that my legs wouldn't give way, that I wouldn't collapse.

After easing myself off the edge of the bed I caught my balance by focusing on taking one step at a time. I made my way to the bathroom and once inside I closed the door before remembering that I couldn't lock it. I stood for a few minutes against the cold hard wood with my eyes closed, trying to gather my thoughts as they scattered around my head.

A few minutes later I found myself in the shower letting the icy-cold water pierce my skin. Although my head was still a mess I knew that I needed to pull it together until I was on my own. With Hugh around I couldn't focus, I couldn't find my way. I was so tangled up in my love for him that I couldn't think clearly and I didn't want to break down again—so, I had to get out of there without him knowing anything was wrong.

When I finally emerged almost an hour later I was shaking on the inside. As I turned the corner into the bedroom I caught a glimpse of Hugh lying across the bed, hugging my pillow. His bare torso was flexed as he tightened his hold on my pillow in his sleep. I leaned against the wall and watched him, feeling my heart melt. This moment in time was exactly where I wanted to stay. The chaos that had plagued me earlier seemed to slip away as I watched him sleep peacefully.

I packed as quietly as I could and dressed quickly before leaning over the bed to kiss his forehead, careful not to wake him. As I turned to pick up my phone from the bedside table I felt his arm wrap around my stomach and pull me back down on to the bed. As soon as my head hit the pillow he climbed on top of me, his mouth enclosed around mine, and the sudden rush of passion burning inside reminded me of all the amazing times we had shared.

As he pulled away, neither one of us wanted to break the connection. We both feared what came next; I knew he would be overseas for a while and wanted to make each moment we were together count. I looked him in the eyes as he leaned over me, and I realised that there was nothing I needed to say, because we were already saying it. I pulled myself up, wrapped my hands around the sides of his face and kissed his forehead before resting my forehead on his. I then extracted myself from his grip and slid off the bed, grabbing my bags and heading for the door.

He followed me out and leaned against the doorframe. As I crossed the threshold he grabbed my wrist, stopping me abruptly.

'I love you, Ava,' he said, the softness in his voice showing he was resigned to the fact that I was fragile and yet still wouldn't tell him why. I knew it was killing him, but there was really nothing more that I could do.

•

I sat in the car silently, looking out the window and feeling my heart shattering into little pieces as I saw the hotel disappear around the corner.

I had fallen down, and even though I couldn't pick myself up I refused to let him help me find my way. My biggest fear was that he would set me on my feet again and without realising it he would then rip the rug out from underneath me—my fragile heart couldn't take it anymore. Part of me longed for the days when I knew nothing more than fun and infatuation, before the complexities of love awakened in my heart and I gave him more than I ever intended to.

When I finally got home all I could do was curl up under my covers and beg for a quick and dreamless sleep to ease the relentless dull ache that throbbed all over my body.

The next few days were painful. I locked myself in my room for the entire weekend and slept; it was the only way to ward off the feelings of depression.

I knew that this situation was ruining me—I had lost the person I was, and yet I didn't have the strength to fight to get her back. I shut myself off from the world, I switched my phone to silent and refused to even look at it. For once in my life I was intent on being selfish . . . I was heading down a dark hole of self-destruction and although I registered every single one of the signs, nothing seemed to be able to pull me out of it.

On Monday morning I got ready for work on autopilot and managed to get out of the house without a problem.

Later in the day I called Hugh from the office. I was really torn up about what I wanted to do, but I just needed to hear his voice.

'Ava, what's wrong?' he said as soon as he picked up. He sounded tired, half-asleep even.

'Hugh, I need to talk to you . . . are you still in bed?' I asked almost accusingly.

'I'm in Europe. I landed about two hours ago. It's two a.m.,' he responded calmly.

'Oh,' I replied, feeling a little guilty that I had stupidly forgotten.

'Are you okay?' he asked almost impatiently.

'I'm fine, Hugh. I'm sorry I woke you. I'll call you later,' I said, chickening out once again.

'Ava, if you need something call me straightaway. It's okay, honestly,' he said, as if he heard the hesitation in my voice.

Hugh messaged me almost every day for the entire month he was overseas, and every time my phone beeped I felt a pang of impatience and frustration at myself, which he copped the brunt of. I knew he was making an effort to help ease my pain but he was unintentionally adding to it. I needed him to open up to me more about his life but I couldn't ask for it. Something had shifted between us, and nothing I did helped me get past it; in turn, everything he did just seemed to aggravate it.

When Hugh flew back into Australia he called me and asked me to meet with him the next week when he flew into town. Resigning myself to the fact that I would only ever find out something when he wanted me to, I decided to give it one more go. I needed to feel that spark, that initial uncomplicated feeling we shared when we connected.

The day he arrived in town he texted me non-stop, telling me his every movement—where he was and what he was doing. I found it odd, but something made me feel like we were taking a step in the right direction.

Another first came for me that day. Hugh was staying out of the city in his beautiful apartment by the beach—the place we had been to many times before and which held so many beautiful memories for me—and he asked me to stay with him, to get away and just spend time alone together, no interruptions, just pure time-out together. He even suggested we make the two-hour car journey together. I jumped at the idea. Something was really different between us; I finally started to feel like there might just be a chance for us, and because of that I allowed myself to be open to the possibility of happiness . . . I allowed myself to trust him unconditionally for the first time in my life.

Getting ready that evening, I felt so excited—as I packed frantically it was almost like this was our first night alone together. The butterflies had returned with full force, and I was blissfully happy. I turned on 'Get Lucky' by Daft Punk, which always put me in a fun, playful mood. For the first time in a long time I was listening to my happy playlist and felt giddy as I sipped on white wine.

An hour later I met Hugh in the city. In an instant I felt myself drawn to him and I almost ran to close the gap between us but I decided to keep a little of the enthusiasm for later. As soon as I reached him he pulled me against him, nuzzling his face into my neck and lifting me off the ground in one swift movement. He cupped his palm to the nape of my neck and leaned me against the car, pushing his entire body against mine, a perfect fit. As usual his kiss was heated, passionate and hungry. He craved me as much as I had always craved him. It drove me wild and I fought the urge to lift up his shirt and run my hands down his back. It was undeniable that we shared more than just a physical attraction . . . it was exactly what I needed to inspire the confidence back into us.

'Ava, this time apart has driven me crazy. I missed you,' he said.

'I know what you mean,' I responded, fighting back the mixed tears of joy and sadness.

We stood there for what felt like forever before he grabbed my luggage and packed it into the car.

As we began our journey I struggled to control the urge to kiss him again. I wanted him, all of him. I had made my decision right then: I was letting go of the past and allowing us a fresh start. It was time for me to prove to Hugh through my actions and words that I really did love him . . . unconditionally.

#ThirtiethConfession

#COAMMPlaylist

'Unconditionally'

Katy Perry

I knew the moment I agreed to go with Hugh that night that something was very different between us. I wasn't sure if we had turned a corner or if it was something else; all I knew was that deep down inside me something had shifted.

During the drive we made plans for a cosy dinner for two and talked about things that were happening in our lives; with each word we spoke I felt the distance that had grown between us close in a little. It wasn't until we stopped along the way to do something as simple as pick up a few groceries that I realised the difference: we were finally in a comfortable and relaxed place with each other. It had taken us almost three years of pain and heartache, but we were finally there.

I wasn't waiting for the other shoe to drop; this time I felt like things were just as they were meant to be . . . perfect.

For the rest of the drive we talked and talked but not about the past—about the future.

When we finally arrived I was high on life, and I needed time to stop and soak in every second of Hugh's presence. As we pulled up and got out of the car the way he looked into my eyes—past everything and straight into my soul—melted my heart. He had never looked at me this way before, and as each second passed in the elevator I felt flashbacks of the best moments we had shared wash over me. I knew then that I was ready to give my whole heart to him. It was the last piece of me I had left and I was ready to give it over with no questions asked.

As we walked into the master bedroom I looked around me and remembered the first time I had slept with him; the time I had given him something that I had never given anyone before. I remembered the nights I was broken and he held me in his arms, not wanting anything beyond making sure I was okay. I remembered the first time he promised me that he wouldn't push my boundaries, and the fact that he had stuck by his promise. I held onto the memories as they took over my mind's eye before I was broken from my reverie when I felt Hugh's hands caress my face and he once again transported me with his kiss. His fingertips burned into my flesh, resonating in my heart before breaking their way through to my soul and lifting me to a place that I had thought only existed in dreams. A place where I was blissfully happy.

As we fell on the bed, wrapped up in everything that we were individually and together, I felt the distance dissolve and a single tear slide down my cheek.

When we surfaced for air it felt like time had stood still. We looked directly, silently into each other's eyes. I studied the features of the man who had captured me in a way no one else ever would. He had saved me from everything that I was, he never took me for granted, he loved me for who I was and because of the way he cared for my fragile heart I knew he really was the one.

'Ava, I'm going to get dinner. How about I pour you a glass of wine, you go and have a nice shower, and we spend the night together . . . just us. What do you say?' he whispered without breaking eye contact.

It was exactly what I needed to hear.

'I'd love to,' I responded before kissing him lightly on the lips.

Standing in the shower twenty minutes later, I felt so refreshed, as if everything I had ever worried about was washing down the drain and I was finally going to be able to begin the next chapter of my life with Hugh. And for the first time since we'd met I didn't care where it was going because I allowed myself to believe that he really did love me, that I was worth everything he was offering. Wherever that took us . . . I was ready.

After dinner we sat on the couch and drank wine while watching television. It was a beautiful, quiet night in while the city below us buzzed on with its Friday-night party. I felt like we were the only people in the world. I lay curled up in Hugh's arm, absent-mindedly sipping my glass of wine, appreciating the seconds that passed while he ran his fingers along the back of my neck and up and down my bare arm until I couldn't take it anymore. I put my glass on the table before returning to my comfortable position and looked directly up at him. He placed his fingertips on my chin and leaned down for a kiss. I was instantly consumed and within seconds found myself slipping underneath him as he climbed on top of me.

He caressed every inch of my body before sliding off my gown and running his hands down my bare stomach. I was desperate to feel him inside me, feel the length of him fill me once again. It wasn't long until my wish was fulfilled and I experienced the most intense sexual experience of my life as we became one again. I felt the deepest connection we had ever shared as he prolonged our mutual climax, lying on the couch wrapped up in each other. His sensual movements were enough to almost send me over the edge as we savoured each other before we climaxed together.

Spent by our emotional and physical connection, he collapsed in my arms, kissing my forehead and cheeks in a way that made me want to express my love for him freely, without pressure or limitation. I loved this man for everything he had ever been to me and everything he had ever done for me.

Wrapped in his arms on the couch later, fresh from another shower, I knew that the next day I would tell him everything I felt and finally give him what he needed. I would tell him what I wanted and where I wanted us to go. And I would tell him how much I truly loved him.

●

It was late by the time I realised I was desperate for bed. Things had been so peaceful and I just wanted to stay in his arms and never move from that spot. Just as I began to drift off to sleep Hugh kissed my forehead, jolting me awake and making me smile.

'Ava, I just have to send an urgent email. After that I'm going to take you off to bed, baby,' he whispered.

I groaned before shifting my position as he leaned over and collected his laptop. I returned to my position in the crook of his arm as he began to write his email. It was the first time he had openly done business around me that I wasn't directly involved with.

I began to drift off again until I heard his fingers leave the keyboard. I thought he had finished until I heard him exhale deeply.

'Have I shown you photos of my granddaughter yet?' he whispered closely to my ear.

My heart stopped. He had never, ever discussed anything like this before, let alone showed me photos of his family. We both knew that I knew about his family but he had never been so open about his life outside of us. I was shocked but excited that he was letting me in after all this time, and I was finally ready to accept him in my life completely.

'No, babe, you haven't,' I said, trying to keep my voice even.

He pulled out his phone, entered his passcode and scrolled through his photos before sharing them with me. We went through at least a hundred different photos from when she was born to a few days before. As he scrolled through the photos I caught a glimpse of his wife, Hayley, holding the baby but he skipped over it and kissed my forehead again. I hugged him tighter; I knew that our situation wasn't ideal but I also knew that if I expected things to change I had to tell him what I wanted.

As he continued to pour out more and more information about his life, I began to feel the tiredness disappear and the longing for him both physically and mentally returned with a vengeance. He was being more open and raw than I had ever experienced, and we were going somewhere we had never been before. I listened intently as he shared memories, about his work or his family, and it wasn't until after 1 a.m. that we finally made our way to bed.

Hugh pulled me off the couch and we walked hand in hand, turning off the lights before climbing into bed.

I exhaled deeply as he wrapped me up in his arms and turned on the television again.

Hugh watched the show intensely as I turned away from the television and searched his face to see what he was thinking. I found myself absent-mindedly drawing lines on his stomach as I rested my head on his chest to hear his heartbeat.

He shifted slightly before kissing the top of my head. I seized the moment to pull myself up and kiss him. As I closed my eyes I felt the electricity run through me when his hands made their way down my now bare back and the tips of his fingers tickled my senses.

Taking charge I gradually slid on top of him without breaking our kiss. I placed my hands on Hugh's chest, gently gliding my nails down towards the band of his jeans. I felt his breath hitch as he sat further back against the headboard when I finally reached my goal. After he removed his last article of clothing I straddled him, eager to feel him inside me again. I was filled with love, joy and hope for the future, which was fuelling the ever-growing desire within me. I positioned him beneath me before sliding down, feeling him fill me deeper than he ever had before. We moved in slow motion together as his mouth made its way down my neck before his lips enclosed around my tender and aroused nipple. I felt his body jerk beneath me as I began to slide down on his thickness once again. He let out a slow, deep groan before grazing his teeth along my collarbone.

I felt raw and exposed at that moment, and I wasn't surprised or disappointed when he flipped me over and took charge.

He looked deeply into my eyes as I felt my climax building with each calculated thrust. I moaned with the deepest of pleasure before the waves of pleasure took over every inch of my body. Within seconds he also gave into his pleasure, crushing his lips against mine so hard that I struggled to fight back tears of joy.

'I love you, Ava,' he whispered with ragged breath as he wrapped me up in the warmth of his arms.

I began to drift off to sleep feeling fulfilled and blessed, so much so that I allowed myself to believe in the possibility that I may just be worthy of a fairytale ending after all.

#Thirty-firstConfession

#COAMMPlaylist
'Ghost'
Ella Henderson

Just before I opened my eyes and faced the day I could instantly tell that I hadn't slept as well as I had hoped. I hadn't moved an inch from the spot in which I had fallen asleep but something deep down told me that something was horribly wrong.

I opened my eyes slowly, feeling Hugh's arms protectively around me, in the hope that I was still dreaming. I had no reason to feel this way and couldn't even put my finger on what it was that I was feeling. After all, I had everything that I had ever wanted. I stirred gently, trying to shake the awful feeling but the only thing I managed to do was wake a peacefully sleeping Hugh. As he woke he tightened his arms around me, squeezing the air out of my lungs with such force

I began to feel dizzy. Then it hit me: the feeling must have been anxiety about finally telling him how I felt. I pondered this thought, trying to make myself believe that that's all that was bothering me.

I felt his lips caress my shoulder before he rolled me over and kissed me intensely.

I felt myself melt against him as he began to travel over my body. My mind grew clouded as we started to make love. I forced myself to push the feeling of dread deep down as the pleasure rippled through me. He knew how to make me feel alive and I knew what I had to do to make things right between us.

'Hugh, before I leave today I need to talk to you,' I whispered breathlessly.

'I know. I can feel it in the air. I know you're ready now,' he said, kissing my cheeks and the tip of my nose. Was he right? Was I truly ready to hand myself over to this man and trust that he was going to do right by me?

There was only one way to find out.

'I'm going to have a shower and then get us some breakfast,' he said. 'Lie here, relax and when you're ready we'll talk.' He kissed me again and then walked into the bathroom.

I stretched luxuriously, savouring the memories of the night before. We had managed to break down so many barriers and he had finally opened up to me in exactly the way that I had wanted for so long. As I heard the shower door close

I snuggled deeper beneath the covers; I could happily have stayed in bed for the rest of the day. A smile crept across my face at the perfect memory we had made just hours earlier, and I found myself imagining a future with Hugh I had never allowed myself to even contemplate before. I wanted Hugh, and it was about time I started to accept that I was going to have him.

As he stepped back into the room I was brought back to reality as his laughter filled the empty space around me.

'Have you been lying there like that the entire time?' he said, chuckling as he began to dress.

'Maybe,' I responded playfully as I undressed him again with my eyes.

'Well, I'm going to grab us something to eat and then I'll be back to feed you and then have my way with you again,' he laughed again.

'Looking forward to it,' I replied with a smile planted firmly on my face as he leaned over and kissed me.

As he left the apartment I grabbed the TV remote control. I wasn't one for daytime television but I was going to take full advantage of the opportunity to do absolutely nothing.

After ten minutes of *Weekend Sunrise* my throat began to burn and I needed a drink of water. I climbed out of bed and half-ran towards the kitchen, still completely naked. I filled my glass with cold water and almost skipped back towards the bedroom, excited for the day ahead. As I passed the lounge room I spotted Hugh's phone connected to the charger lying on the floor.

'Oh shit, he's left his phone,' I said out loud. His phone was the one thing Hugh was never without—in his position he couldn't afford to leave it behind in case any of his clients needed to get in touch for something important.

As I walked back into the bedroom a wave of nausea swept over me. I felt my body begin to shake, and suddenly I knew I had to go back out into the lounge room—to Hugh's phone. I was at a complete loss as to why I had to do this, but I followed my instinct.

'Get a fucking grip, Ava,' I said to myself, but I still hurried to collect my robe from the bedroom floor and threw it around my shoulders as I walked back through to the lounge room.

I saw it again . . . his phone.

The feeling in the pit of my stomach took over again as I slowly walked towards it. The world around me faded to black as I stood in front of the one thing that held all of Hugh's secrets. I bent down to pick it up and felt my heart begin to race and my hands began to shake. I had never been the kind of person to go through someone else's phone, but something deep inside me told me that the answers to all of my concerns and questions lay in the little black device now burning hotly in my hand.

I closed my eyes, trying to make sense of what was happening. With my eyes shut tightly I saw the images of the night before play out in front of me, then I remembered how different everything between us had felt. He had offered up more information to me in the past twenty-four hours than over the past two and a bit years, and that scared me more than I cared to admit. When he was evasive I could handle it, but he had changed the game the moment he opened his life up to me. The combination code to his phone flashed before my eyes and I knew then that I needed to follow my gut instinct.

I opened my eyes slowly and slid my finger across the screen. Up popped the security-code request and before I could stop myself I was entering the same combination he had typed the night before.

It unlocked and the home screen flashed before me. My heartbeat quickened as I hit the messages icon and began to slowly scroll through the messages.

I clicked on the first name I saw and my whole world crashed down around me. I dropped to the floor as the ground tore out from beneath me. My heart shattered into a million pieces, and my head was flooded with visions I would never be able to forget. I closed the message immediately before my eyes caught more and more of the same type of thing with so many different women. I saw the messages—sexts—back and forth, and images of the women in all types of positions. My mind failed to register that I was seeing more of the female anatomy than I had ever in my life, even taking into account the fact that I am a woman. I was overcome by the feeling of utter betrayal as I dropped the phone and watched it fall in slow motion to the floor. For a while time stood still, and I felt nothing but a roaring numbness. I then felt bile rise in my throat and I ran towards the bathroom in time to expel the contents of my stomach. I sat on the cold marble floor, shaking uncontrollably while an unimaginably excruciating pain consumed my body and violent tears ran down my cheeks with no sign of stopping. My head began to throb with a headache that teetered on the edge of white blinding pain. Stars fogged my vision as I tried to fight the crippling agony, all the while a voice in my head screamed, *I told you so!*—and I realised the voice was my own. I closed my eyes in the hope of slowing my breath, which hitched every time I inhaled, as if my body was on repeat.

There was nothing I could do to stop any of it. I couldn't muster the ability to hate him at that point. All I wanted to do was knock myself out and hope to god that it was all a dream . . . reality seemed too cruel to handle. I wanted to run, hide and pretend it was happening to someone else. I really wasn't ready to deal with the fact that Hugh, *my* Hugh, had committed an unforgivable act of betrayal. It was worse than anything I had been forced to endure in my early years. Somewhere deep down I had known that this was coming. I had known that something was wrong, I had felt it deep within my soul, but I had forced my concerns aside for the sake of my love for Hugh, and somehow I was still shocked. I felt an impending numbness encroaching, and I prayed for it to set in, to take me over and protect me, but this was my consequence, this was my punishment for agreeing to be his mistress—he had cheated on me as he had cheated on his wife.

I knew I would never forget the vivid images of the naked women on his phone, making a lie of every word he had spoken to me for so many years, and every moment we had spent together—it made me feel like a cheap, dirty whore. I was disgusted with myself for falling for someone so deeply to whom clearly I was easily—and frequently—replaceable.

I suddenly lurched back to reality as I remembered that he was going to return shortly and was expecting something I was no longer willing to give him. I couldn't comprehend being in the same room as him, and I had no idea how I was going to handle the situation. I felt utterly destroyed and I knew that it was of my own doing. I blamed myself for lowering my guard and allowing Hugh to break me.

When I finally pulled myself up off the floor I cried harder than I ever had. What the fuck was I going to do now?

I ran myself a shower. I couldn't control the tears and I was too tired to care. As I stood under the shower I felt the cold hard reality of my situation rage around me. I went through every possible emotion and was left reeling from them all. The hurt turned to betrayal until the sickness returned as I came to the conclusion that countless other women must have stood in the same shower in which I was now crying my heart out. I flung myself forward and hit the glass door, trying to distance myself from that reality. I grabbed the closest towel, turned off the water and ran into the bedroom, where I frantically packed. I needed to get out before he returned. I couldn't be anywhere near him; I was afraid of what I would do if I ran into him. I was afraid that I would black out and lash out at him or worse—I would make excuses for him and forgive him.

I dressed as quickly as I could, trying my hardest not to touch the bed in which we had created so many memories; the same bed in which he had taken my virginity, an act that had meant so much to me but now sickened me as I realised that many other women had shared the same bed with him. I still felt dirty, and no amount of scrubbing myself clean would change this feeling. It was eating my skin and I was sure that it would never disappear.

As I finished packing and grabbed the handle on my suitcase I heard the elevator arrive and the front door click as he entered. I panicked and threw myself on the bed, trying my hardest to control the tremors running through me. I contemplated jumping off the balcony just to avoid him, but I knew it wasn't possible. I wasn't ready to confront him but I couldn't ignore the situation either. I was furious about everything, including the fact that I didn't know what to do. My pounding headache returned while I sat pretending to watch television as he walked into the room, leaned down and kissed my cheek. I flinched at his touch, too shocked to speak.

'Hey, baby, sorry I took so long. I'll get breakfast sorted for you and leave it on the table when you're ready. I didn't expect to see you dressed,' he said, smiling and caressing my shoulder with this fingertips. I remained where I was, frozen. I wasn't going to do this, I wasn't going to let it go but I needed to get my head straight before I confronted him.

'I'll be out soon,' I said, trying to curb the frostiness in my tone.

He walked out of the bedroom and I collapsed within myself. I didn't want to eat, I didn't even want to breathe.

I made sure that everything was packed in my bags and positioned them near the door, within easy reach if I wanted to grab them and leave quickly.

When I finally walked out into the dining room I saw Hugh sitting on the balcony—the place he had taken me by surprise and awakened my sexual world for the first time. He was reading the newspaper while talking to one of his clients on the same phone that had just proved to me that he was a cheater.

I saw the food sitting on the table with a glass of orange juice, and I sat down to try it. I took a bite but instantly wanted to throw up. I forced myself to swallow, picking at the egg before I threw it in the garbage.

As he walked into the kitchen I was filling my glass with water, trying my hardest to keep calm and steady myself, but despite my best efforts he knew something was wrong.

'Ava?' he said in a calm and soothing voice.

I dropped the glass in the kitchen sink and stuck my finger up at him as I walked towards the bedroom again. I didn't know what else to do, I knew I was falling apart but I needed to hold it together and get out of there.

'Ava!' he called after me.

'Leave me alone, Hugh!' I screamed back. He didn't follow. As I turned the corner into the bedroom I saw him standing with his head in his hands, at a loss.

As I grabbed my handbag and suitcase I heard his phone ring, and I thought to myself that it must be one of his whores . . . then I realised I was one of them too. A sharp pain erupted in my stomach, forcing me to keel over. I caught my breath before making myself stand upright. It was time for me to leave. I needed to breathe again, I needed to break down in solitude.

As I walked out of the bedroom with my bags, the pain rippled through my body again. I couldn't believe that such an incredible night had ended in a way that would change me for the rest of my life. I wanted to crumble to the floor and let the pain consume me. The man I had trusted with my heart, my soul, my body and my life had shattered my world in the blink of an eye. I couldn't bear to look at him, I couldn't bear to be in the same universe as him. I was blinded by my love for him and it had cost me more than I had thought I had wagered—in the game of love I had gambled my heart and lost in such a way that I wasn't sure I would be able to put the pieces back together. I was broken.

I carried my bags to the front door, crippled with fear and desperately hoping I wouldn't stumble, because I was afraid I wouldn't be able to get back up. I placed my hand on the door handle and heard his voice as he spoke to his assistant. I turned and took one final look at him until I couldn't stand it anymore; he looked at me with utter confusion and stopped speaking as tears began to stream down my face again. I turned, pulled down the handle and heard the familiar click of the door opening. I tugged it towards me and crossed the threshold. I heard him yell, 'Fuck!' as the door closed behind me and I stood in the hallway struggling to breathe. I prayed that he wouldn't come after me, I prayed that he would stay in the apartment and never contact me again.

I knew that if I turned around at that moment in time I wouldn't be able to walk away; I knew that I would fall into his arms and shake uncontrollably as the tears fell for what would surely be an eternity. I knew if I stayed . . . it would kill me. I had already lost so much just by being with him, and the only thing I had left to lose was my sanity. As I watched the elevator make its way to the penthouse I saw out of the corner of my eye the door to the apartment being yanked open. I couldn't even look at him.

'Ava, what the fuck is going on?' he asked with a hint of panic in his voice. I turned and looked at him with a blank stare, feeling empty. I had nothing left to say but I forced out the only words I could muster.

'I can't be near you right now, Hugh, I have to go.'

Before he could say anything the elevator arrived. I hurried in and pressed the button for the ground floor before punching the 'close door' button repeatedly. Just as the elevator doors closed he ran to stop them but he was too late.

I slumped to the floor and allowed the debilitating pain to finally take over every corner of my body and soul as reality set in. The same statement kept playing in my mind: surely this is enough . . . surely this is what I need to be able to walk away.

I sat there telling myself 'It is over . . . forever.' I felt humiliated. How was I going to explain this to everyone around me?

Acknowledgements

Writing this book has been a dream come true for me. There have been so many people who have helped to make this dream a reality.

First I would like to thank my family. Mum, thank you for being my everything, for sacrificing so much and for being there to help me pick up the pieces when I let you in. I owe you everything.

Nan, you are the reason that I get up every morning with a smile on my face. You are the greatest first memory that anyone can ever have. Words cannot express how much I love and appreciate you for being a rock when I didn't feel I could turn to anyone else.

Dad, I remember the first Father's Day gift I ever bought you—it was a mug that said you were the World's Greatest Dad, but I never really believed that. You are the greatest dad in the universe. Thank you for being there for me even when I didn't want you to be. I love you.

To my beloved grandfather: you are the greatest man to have ever walked this planet. My biggest regret in life is that I will never get the chance to tell you this again. You have been the benchmark for any man who enters my life, and words will never explain how much you helped me grow and how safe you made me feel as a child in a world full of pain. I hope I have made you proud.

Maria: without you I would never have made it through this life. I can honestly say that you have been one of the biggest and most influential people in my life, the big sister I never had and the only person I would ever listen to when times got hard. You have been my rock and one of the greatest sources of pride in my life, the other half of my craziness and most of all the best friend I could ever have asked for. I will love you as long as I live, and beyond that. Shine bright like a diamond, princess!

To CoCo: you will never know how much our late night chats meant to me. I can never say enough how lucky I am to have a best friend like you who is always there to pick up the pieces when my mind just can't seem to function anymore; for always supplying me with energy drinks to make sure that I finished my book on time. Thank you for being you . . . never change.

To the entire team at Allen & Unwin: I really cannot thank you all enough. A huge thankyou must go to Claire Kingston for putting up with my overly cautious nature when it came to my anonymity and for believing in my story, even working while you were getting married halfway across the world. I cannot express my gratitude in words.

To Kathryn and Claire, the two wonderful editors who read over my book and made the number of changes that at times must have been tiring to do, not to mention having to sit through my constant emotional backflips, which I am quite sure left you more than confused throughout the book . . . trust me, I really was that conflicted!

To the fans who've followed my story along the way: I really cannot say how amazing it is to be sitting here writing this dedication to you all. Thank you for allowing me to share my life and experiences with you. Without you, none of this would be possible.

Lastly, to Hugh: I will always love you, in this life and the next.

Ava Reilly is a young Australian woman. By day she works in public relations. By night she writes her much-loved 'Confessions of a Millionaire's Mistress' blog. This is her first book.